Classic Kosher Cooking

simply
delicious

winning recipes for every day and holidays

SARA FINKEL

Classic Kosher Cooking

simply delicious

winning recipes for every day and holidays

KTAV PUBLISHING HOUSE

SARA FINKEL

First published 2009
Copyright © 2009 by Sara Finkel
ISBN 978-1-56871-479-0

Printing year 2017
Published and Distributed by:
KTAV PUBLISHING HOUSE
527 Empire Blvd.
Brooklyn,NY 11225
Ph:718-972-5449 Fax: 718-972-6307
Email: orders@ktav.com
Website:www.ktav.com

Printed in China

This cookbook is dedicated
with affection
to my very devoted children,
my sons and my
daughters-in-law

CONTENTS

APPETIZERS

SOUPS

FISH

VEGETABLES

KUGELS

KUGELS (CONTD.)

PASTA, RICE & TOFU

CHALLAH & BREAD

DESSERTS

CAKES & ICINGS

COOKIES & BARS

PASTRIES, PIES & CHEESECAKES

MICROWAVE COOKING

PESACH

ACKNOWLEDGMENTS

Each of us is connected to others, dependent upon them in the many facets of his or her life. I would, therefore, like to acknowledge with deep appreciation those who have been of assistance to me in preparing this cookbook:

To Miriam Zakon, former editor-in-chief of Targum Press. I am grateful to her for her projected confidence in the success of this cookbook, as she so eagerly discussed producing another *Classic Kosher Cooking* and arranged for it to be published by Targum.

My profound appreciation to Rabbi and Mrs. Mordechai Plaut. Rabbi Plaut was the editor of the English edition of *Yated Ne'eman* newspaper, and gave me the opportunity to write the food column for the past six years. Many of the recipes and articles in this book originally appeared in the weekly edition of that newspaper. My thanks to Devora Plaut for so efficiently proofreading my column.

To my dear cousin Roberta Farber, who so willingly edited some of my articles with great efficiency. Her profound writing ability and erudition is matched by her genuinely warm and giving personality. My heartfelt appreciation to you, Roberta, for your kindness and for being such a good friend.

It has been, indeed, a special privilege for me to work with Ita Olesker, chief editor of *Classic Kosher Cooking: Simply Delicious*. My profoundest gratitude to you, Ita, for your excellent editing, as well as the efficient and courteous assistance you gave me.

My deep appreciation to Beena Sklare, the graphic artist at Targum, for her beautiful book and cover design. And to all of the dedicated staff at Targum Press — Bracha, Michal, Chaya Baila, Debbie, Bassi, and Allison, and everyone else who was involved in this cookbook. I truly thank you for a job well done.

I would like to pay special tribute to the memory of Rabbi Moshe Dombey, *zt"l*, founder of Targum Press, who encouraged me to write a cookbook. *Classic Kosher Cooking* was the outcome, and it turned out to be a bestseller. I am grateful for the assistance provided me.

To my daughters-in-law, Leah and Mimi, who are constantly at my side always with encouragement and support in so many ways. I want to thank them for answering every "beck and call" when I needed them — selecting and reviewing some of the recipes and articles as well as helping me with the testing. With affection I wholeheartedly thank both of you.

My heartfelt appreciation to my devoted sons, who are a continued source of advice and encouragement to me in my various endeavors. Gedalia motivated me to carry out the laborious task of writing another cookbook at this particular time. When things appeared to become overwhelming and time-consuming, he encouraged me to continue, saying repeatedly, "Mom, you're performing a public service — carry on."

My thanks to Marilyn Carmen, who so graciously edited some of the articles.

With deep appreciation to Shulamit Boncheck, an exemplary homemaker, who reviewed some of the recipes and also shared two or three of her own.

Thanks to Yocheved Engel, a regular member of our Tuesday morning *shiur*, who graciously edited some of the articles in the early stages of this work. Thank you also to Chanie Newhouse for your efficient help at the computer.

I would like express a special thank you to my two good neighbors, Yocheved Meth and Leah Ben Porat, whom I consider to be computer experts. Each time I got stuck at the computer and hollered for help, they so willing rushed up and helped me out. My sincere gratitude to Aviva Durant, another expert with the computer, who assisted me so readily when a technical problem came up, as well as in other ways.

I would like to say *todah rabbah* to my beloved granddaughters, all *n'shei b'nei Torah*, for testing some of the recipes for me as well as sharing some of their own. They did it with joy and willingness and made me feel it was a family endeavor, which meant so much to me. "Bubbie, *zeh mishpachti*," they exclaimed. Thank you, my darlings, for your help as well as for your inspiration. And, most of all, thank you for being my granddaughters.

I would like to thank the many readers of my first book, *Classic Kosher Cooking,* for the marvelous feedback they keep giving me, which gave me the encouragement to write a second book.

I would like to pay tribute to the memory of my husband, Rabbi Eliahu Meyer Finkel, *zt"l,* for the devotion and encouragement he showed in my endeavors, as well as the lofty principles he had in perpetuating our heritage.

With humility, I would like to express my most profound *hakaras hatov* to HaKadosh Baruch Hu, whose *siyatta d'Shmaya* I felt throughout the preparation of this book. It is only He who endowed me with the ability, perseverance, understanding, and strength to be able carry out this time-consuming endeavor.

Sara Finkel
Jerusalem, 5769

INTRODUCTION

I n keeping with the theme of my first cookbook, *Classic Kosher Cooking*, I hope that this new cookbook too will make us aware of the spiritual value of cooking and the elevated role which we women have been granted.

Often, we think of cooking for our family and guests as an endless chore. True, there are many time-consuming details involved: shopping for food, cleaning vegetables and fowl, serving, and finally cleaning up and putting things away. All of this takes time and effort.

But let us consider that it is the attitude we have towards our work that is most important. It is our perception that really determines our attitude, and by having the right attitude we can avoid the feeling of pressure that these tasks create. As Jewish women, let us not regard our responsibilities as a burden, but rather as a *zechus*, a merit that we have dating from the time of *matan Toraseinu*.

In *Sefer Shemos, Parashas Pekudei*, we learn of the building of the Mishkan, the Tabernacle, which was erected with the contributions of *b'nei Yisrael*. Each person gave of his possessions according to his desire and hoped that his contribution would be designated for the construction of the holiest parts of the Mishkan.

Betzalel, the great architect who constructed the Mishkan, perceived through his prophetic vision the emotions that accompanied each contribution. The contributions of those who gave with their whole hearts were designated for the construction of the *Kodesh HaKodashim*, the holiest part of the Mishkan. The contributions of those who gave more reluctantly or with reservations went towards the building of a lesser part of this holy edifice, such as the courtyard and its structure.

As a homemaker, it is important that in your life and in your work you seek to emulate those who gave to the construction of the Mishkan with a full heart. Our Sages emphasize how important this is in a powerful Talmudic statement: "As long as the Temple stood, the altar wrought atonement for Israel, but today, the table of a person becomes the *Mizbe'ach*" (*Berachos* 55a). This means that the table in each of our homes can atone for our sins. It is we, the Jewish women, who are responsible for these tables. By being careful with what we put on our tables and doing our elevated work with a whole heart, we can accrue many merits for our homes and our families.

Equally important to preparing food is creating the right atmosphere. We must seek to create an atmosphere of harmony, contentment, and especially gratitude to Hashem in our homes. For as much as the food we present makes others feel welcome, it is ultimately the joy with which we serve it that truly gladdens their hearts.

I like to think that this cookbook will not only provide you with recipes for foods to put on your table, but will also make you more aware of the great *zechus* with which women have been endowed — the *zechus* of giving. I hope it will help you understand that the many seemingly mundane tasks we perform gain a measure of *kedushah,* sanctity, when we perform them with a happy heart.

Let us be grateful for the great *zechus* with which we have been blessed. We have the privilege of contributing to the sustenance, joy, health, and welfare of those who are dear to us, through the art of cooking and baking and through the mitzvah of *hachnasas orchim* — welcoming guests to our table throughout the week, and especially on Shabbos and *yamim tovim.*

SHABBOS
& HOLIDAYS

SHABBOS & HOLIDAYS

The Talmud teaches that the Roman Emperor came to visit Rabbi Yehudah HaNasi on Shabbos. He enjoyed the food so much, even though it was somewhat cold, that he returned again one day during the week. This time the food was nice and hot, but it did not taste as good. He asked his host why the food was so much tastier on Shabbos, and Rabbi Yehudah HaNasi answered, "The reason you enjoyed the food more then was because it had a special spice — it's called Shabbos."

Shabbos is like a sparkling gem to the Jewish people. It transforms the simplest home into a palace, imbuing it with blessings and sanctity.

Since meals for Shabbos should be particularly festive, the most succulent food is prepared for this day. No monetary expense is incurred when we buy food and drink in honor of Shabbos, since our Sages tell us that if someone cannot afford to prepare substantial meals for Shabbos, he must borrow the money he needs and Hashem will return it to him.

When we think of preparing food for Shabbos, we invariably think of cholent. In the years around the turn of the century and earlier, women made cholent at home, labeled their pot, and then brought it to the town bakery on *erev Shabbos* to cook slowly overnight in the oven there. After services in the synagogue, the older children would stop at the bakery, where the inviting aroma filled the air, to bring home their pot. Kiddush was made, and the family and guests sat down to a delicious, piping-hot cholent.

MOTZA'EI SHABBOS

King David knew that his end was to come on a Shabbos. Therefore, in gratitude for each Shabbos that he was granted life, he celebrated by making an elaborate feast on *motza'ei Shabbos,* a *melaveh malkah.* In partaking of this *motza'ei Shabbos seudah,* one should recite, "This is the *seudah* of King David."

Just as a festive meal is prepared upon wishing farewell to an important guest, the *melaveh malkah* is served in honor of the outgoing Shabbos Queen and should therefore be served in a festive atmosphere. The table should be covered with a cloth, and some have a custom to light candles. It is a time for inviting guests and singing songs, things that add to the gaiety of the occasion.

Though we are required to eat only a *kezayis,* an olive-sized serving of food, a special dish should be prepared for this fourth meal of Shabbos. It is customary to eat some form of heated bread, such as French toast or toast, and include that in the dishes to be prepared. Rashi states that a hot drink at the conclusion of Shabbos serves as a *refuah,* a source of healing.

The food that we eat at the *melaveh malkah* meal nourishes both our bodies and our souls. A bone in the human body located at the top of the vertebrae, called the *luz* in Hebrew, derives its nourishment only from the *melaveh malkah seudah.* The *luz* bone is the only bone that remains intact in the body even after death, because it is necessary for achieving *techias hameisim,* resurrection, and therefore must exist at the coming of *Mashiach.*

(Based on excerpts from the *Mishnah Berurah* and *Siddur HaGra.*)

ROSH HASHANAH

How effective is a word? A word's influence can reach as far as the upper spheres. On Rosh Hashanah, words and symbols affect the events and the fate of the entire year.

On this *yom tov,* we eat symbolic foods to remind us that man stands before the True Judge and needs to repent. The custom of eating these foods, which revolves around a play on words, originates in a

Talmudic passage in the Gemara in *Rosh HaShanah* and is later clarified in the *Shulchan Aruch*. This custom reflects our fears and hopes at this significant time of the year and is our attempt to do whatever possible to ensure a favorable decree. We combine the power of the meanings of these symbolic foods with the power of prayer by reciting the appropriate supplication with each food. The *Yehi Ratzon* is essential, as it strengthens the power of the *siman*, the symbolic food, and helps bring it to fruition. Our prayers sanctify these foods, making them a source of holiness and a means of awakening us to repentance.

In the same way that we make the positive effort to eat certain foods, we avoid eating nuts on Rosh HaShanah because the numerical value of the Hebrew term for nut, *egoz*, is the same as the numerical value of the word *chet*, sin.

On Rosh HaShanah, it is customary to eat sweet foods made with honey and sugar, and to avoid sharp or sour foods such as horseradish, pickles, and lemons.

Rabbi Yisrael Salanter, *zt"l*, the founder of the Mussar Movement, told his children to curb their anger on the night of Rosh HaShanah, and that this would be stronger than any of the symbols, because this is the time when the Book of Life is open and we are being judged for our behavior. That is the reason why we say the *Yehi Ratzon*s during the evening meal: We want to remind ourselves of what is going on in the higher spheres. At this time, our hearts should be filled with love for our fellowman as well as with goodness and joy towards our family as we gather around the festive table with our dear ones on Rosh HaShanah.

Some of the Symbolic Foods and Their Meanings

- Apple: We dip a slice of apple in honey and ask Hashem for a sweet year.

- Pomegranates: Just as the pomegranate has many seeds, we ask to be granted countless merits on Rosh HaShanah when our judgment for the year is being decided.

- Carrots and black-eyed peas: Carrot is called *mehren* in Yiddish, and black-eyed peas are *rubia* in Aramaic. Both mean "many." These foods are symbolic of the many merits we ask for on this day, as our destiny is being determined.

- Head of fish: We eat from the head of the fish because it symbolizes the hope that we be like the head — the part that controls our instincts — and not like the tail, which is passive and reflexive. *Lerosh,* "[like] a head," is an acronym for "may it be the will of our Father in Heaven."

- Fish: Fish are a symbol of fruitfulness. We pray that we will multiply like the fish in the sea. Rashi says there is no *ayin hara,* evil eye, associated with fish, as their eyes are always open and watchful.

- Dates: *Tamar,* the Hebrew word for date, is related to the Hebrew word for "to eliminate." We ask Hashem to eliminate our enemies — especially the enemy within us, the *yetzer hara,* the evil inclination.

- Crookneck squash: Squash in Hebrew is *k'ra,* which means "to tear." We pray that all evil decrees be torn up.

- Spinach or beet green: *Silka,* Aramaic for beets or spinach, is related to the Hebrew word that means "to remove," and alludes to the hope that our enemies be removed.

SUKKOS

The Rambam teaches that the reason we dwell in a fragile sukkah for seven days is in order to remember the difficult times in our days of prosperity. This holiday emphasizes the importance of living a modest life. We leave our elegant homes to live in the fragile sukkah because it is reminiscent of our ancestors' life in the desert, a life that lacks comfort and convenience.

 The sukkah's tenuous structure reminds us that it is not our homes that shelter us, but our trust and faith in Hashem, our true Shield and Protector. It symbolizes that everything material is only temporary and transient, while our spiritual accomplishments last for eternity. The sturdy walls and flimsy roof of the sukkah remind us of the nature of man — firm in his beliefs and practices, yet humble and always mindful of the Higher Power above.

Sukkos is also the harvest holiday, known as the Festival of the Ingathering — *Chag HaAsif*. To symbolize our bounty, it is customary to serve stuffed foods — stuffed cabbage, stuffed peppers, a variety of strudels. Chol HaMoed is also an important part of Sukkos and should be treated as a holiday, by serving special foods, dressing in our *yom tov* finery, and visiting family and friends. If Shabbos falls on Chol HaMoed, many housewives prepare two kugels — one for Shabbos and one for Chol HaMoed.

When partaking of our meals in the sukkah, remember only attractive serving pieces should be brought in, such as the elegant soup tureen and silver platters you save for special occasions. Use your better set of china which you use on Shabbos.

The last day of Sukkos, which is Hoshana Rabbah, marks the final sealing of the Divine decrees issued on Yom Kippur, and on this day we enjoy our last meal in the sukkah.

CHANUKAH

The mitzvah of *ner Chanukah*, kindling the lights of Chanukah, is a precious mitzvah that we are careful to fulfill properly. The Rambam points out that even if a person is very poor and must choose between buying wine for Kiddush on Shabbos or buying oil to light the Chanukah lights, buying oil for Chanukah takes precedence.

The small vial of undefiled oil found in the Beis HaMikdash was only enough to burn for one day, but it miraculously lasted for eight days. This miracle was understood as a sign that Hashem was pleased with the Jewish people's opposition to the materialism, idolatry, and the physically oriented mindset that was imposed upon them by the Greeks. The oil we use to light the menorah represents this miracle, and with this mitzvah we remind ourselves of the spiritual strength that prevailed at that time and which we pray we will be able to emulate for all time.

The culinary representation of this miracle is the eating of foods fried in oil, such as latkes (pancakes) made from potatoes, cheese, zucchini, or apple and nut, and doughnuts that are deep-fried in oil, known in Israel as *sufganiyot*. In Israel, it is customary to eat *sufganiyot* throughout the winter months.

A second culinary custom is to prepare dairy foods, in commemoration of the deeds of the brave heroine, Yehudis. Yehudis gave Helifornes, the Syrian general who wanted to conquer Jerusalem and our people, large quantities of cheese to eat and wine to drink. In accordance with her plan, he soon became drunk and fell asleep. She then killed him and brought about a great victory for our nation. It is this that we remember as we prepare and eat dairy dishes.

In publicizing the miracle of the oil and in reciting *Hallel*, we express our *hakaros hatov,* our gratitude to Hashem, for the many miracles He performs for us each day and for the kindnesses that he shows us in so many ways.

PURIM

The preparation of a variety of foods plays an important role in the joyous holiday of Purim. The Purim *seudah* begins in the afternoon of the holiday and lasts until well after sunset. This *seudas mitzvah* commemorates the feast that Queen Esther prepared, that resulted in the salvation of the Jewish people and prevented their annihilation by the wicked Haman.

On Purim, costumed children can be seen throughout the streets carrying gifts of food, *mishloach manos,* to friends and neighbors, in order to express the brotherly love engendered by Queen Esther and Mordechai HaTzaddik amongst the Jewish people of Shushan. To fulfill the mitzvah of *mishloach manos,* one must send two kinds of ready-to-eat foods to at least one friend. Another important mitzvah of the day is *matanos l'evyonim,* gifts to the poor. This mitzvah is fulfilled by giving a gift of money to two needy people.

Purim is a *chag* when the *balebusta* can go all-out in preparing her favorite dishes and various kinds of foods to enhance this joyous festival.

If you prepare something homemade to put in your *mishloach manos,* it would be an extra bonus to include the recipe as well. Whichever way you do it, the most important thing is to experience the joy of giving — the joy of Purim.

PESACH

In the weeks before Pesach, most of us find ourselves occupied with the cleaning out of *chametz*, a seemingly mundane task that makes us both busy and exhausted. Some even resent the burdens of this apparently trivial preoccupation, with all of its details, especially the arduous job of cleaning the refrigerator and scrubbing the stove.

But a great Torah scholar tells us that this concern for so-called trivia — the most minute details — is the very reason that the Jewish woman is so exceptional. The special role of the Jewish woman in the world of Torah is not necessarily to be concerned with the grand tasks of life that garner attention and praise. Her role, especially while preparing for Pesach, is to be concerned with the small things of this world, the parts of life that shallow people deem "trivial."

If you stop to think, the mitzvos themselves are concerned with the "smaller" things of life — the various *berachos* over food, buying a new garment, taking *challah*, lighting candles, visiting a sick person, etc. For the most part, the Torah is not concerned with life-altering actions and decisions; these are ultimately dealt with by Hashem. It is how we handle our simple day-to-day tasks that is relevant. The Torah is concerned with sanctifying the mundane because it is these very small things of life, with which women are particularly involved, that lead to purity, sanctity, and holiness.

A woman's strength, says this *gadol ba Torah*, lies in the small things she does, and keeping this in mind as we prepare for Pesach will elevate our *avodah* and transform it into something deep and meaningful.

SHAVUOS

Shavuos marks the time when we received the Torah, *zeman matan Toraseinu*. "Just as the apples appear on the apple tree fifty days after its blossoms sprout, so too, *klal Yisrael* received the Torah fifty days after leaving bondage in Egypt" (*Pesikta Zutresa*). When the Jewish people were about to receive the Torah at Mount Sinai after leaving Egypt, they encamped at the bottom of the mountain, united, as one person, with one heart. This unity was essential, since the Torah could only be received in such an atmosphere.

Unity is manifested in various ways, but it is always expressed as concern for others, such as when one shares his possessions or abilities in order to make another's task lighter. In unity there is strength. Indeed, the Shechinah can only rest upon a people who are united. Among the many ways in which the homemaker contributes to this all-important unity is *hachnasas orchim* — the welcoming spirit and the tasty meals she prepares for her family and all others who grace her table. When a woman gives of herself by bringing together family and friends and preparing and serving special delicacies to enhance the *yom tov* of Shavuos, she embraces this *achdus,* this unity.

Unlike other Jewish holidays where meat dishes generally predominate, on Shavuos we eat dairy dishes as well. Indeed, *milchig* dining has come a long way from the time when our grandmothers were toddlers. Blintzes, for example, were originally filled with cheese of a savory or mildly sweetened flavor. Today we stuff paper-thin *bletlach* (blintz leaves) with tuna, kasha, sautéed vegetables, sliced mushrooms, or creamy mashed potatoes. They can even be served for dessert, filled with cherry or blueberry pie filling, a combination of apple and nuts, cubed mango with coconuts, or fresh sliced strawberries with whipped cream. I don't recall Grandma entertaining the idea of dessert blintzes or no-bake cheesecake, *milchig* moussaka, and the many other new dairy gastronomical delights which we enjoy in the twenty-first century.

However, let us keep uppermost in our minds the true significance of Shavuos, which is that it marks the time when we acquired our most important and dearest possession — the holy Torah. The Torah is our blueprint for life, our guide for a better connection with one another and with the One Above. It is our guide to life in this world, a world in which our actions will ultimately affect the next world — the real world — after *meah v'esrim shanah*, 120 years.

ROSH CHODESH

Rosh Chodesh was given especially to the women, because the women in *klal Yisrael* did not contribute their jewelry to the golden calf. And indeed it is a special day. On this day it is a mitzvah to have a sumptuous meal, usually with meat, and to include in Birkas HaMazon the special paragraph *Yaaleh VeYavo*, which is said on *yamim tovim.* When we recite *Hallel* on Rosh Chodesh, we say, "This is the day which Hashem has made, let us rejoice and be happy on it."

Our Sages tell us that Rosh Chodesh is among the three special days when one should not hesitate to spend more money for food for family and guests. Even though many women are forced to be frugal with their food budget, this should not apply on Rosh Chodesh. One should not skimp, but rather go all out to obtain the best in order to prepare delicious foods for this special day.

SUGGESTED MENUS

SHABBOS FRIDAY NIGHT MEAL

Special Whole Wheat Challah (p. 139)
Traditional Gefilte Fish (p. 3) with Horseradish
Eggplant Marinade (p. 36)
Classic Chicken Soup (p. 21) with Fluffiest Matzah Balls (p. 245)
Chicken Gourmet (p. 43) or Stuffed Breast of Veal (p. 67)
Zahavale's Onion Kugel (p. 114)
Pecan Toss Salad (p. 38)
Chocolate Mousse Dessert (p. 156)

SHABBOS DAYTIME MEAL

Halibut Salad (p. 5)
Red Cabbage Salad (p. 34)
Classic Cholent with Kishke (p. 70)
Stuffed Chicken Cutlets (p. 47)
Tangy Vegetable Salad (p. 37)
Almond Crumb Topped Ice Cream (p. 151)

SEUDAH SHELISHIS

Mock Chopped Herring (p. 17) or Avocado-Herring Spread (p. 18)
Vegetable Trifle (p. 39)
Mimi's Baked Fish Patties (p. 80)
Malkie's Ice Cream Supreme, Pistachio Flavor (p. 150)
Orange Juice Cake (p. 174)

ROSH HASHANAH NIGHT MEAL

Chicken Livers with Pineapple Tidbits (p. 13)
Pumpkin Soup (p. 25)
Crunchy Carrot Salad (p. 33)
Honeyed Roast Beef with Sweet Potatoes (p. 55) or Shulamit's
    Chicken with Sweet Potatoes (p. 46)
Special Zucchini Kugel (p. 113)
Honey Orange Date Cake (p. 168)
Cherry Crumb Pie (p. 224)

SUKKOS MENU

Eggplant Roulade (p. 8)
Pecan Toss Salad (p. 38)
Potted Roast Beef (p. 56)
Cantonese Brown Rice with Vegetables (p. 128)
Cauliflower Polonaise (p. 101)
Raspberry-Nut Strudel (p. 216)

CHANUKAH MENU

Mock Chopped Liver (p. 16)
Creamy Onion Soup (p. 28)
Baked Fish in Tomato Sauce (p. 77)
Tangy Vegetable Salad (p. 37)
Tri-Colored Pashtida (p. 117)
Vegetable Latkes (p. 119)
Apple-Nut Latkes (p. 120)

PURIM MENU

Chicken Fricassee (p. 13)
Cream of Mushroom Soup (p. 23)
Red Cabbage Salad (p. 34)
Roast Beef with Delicious Sweet and Sour Sauce (p. 57)
Yom Tov Chicken (p. 45)
Broccoli Souffle (p. 96)
Noodle Kugellettes (p. 109)
Almond Crumb Topped Ice Cream (p. 151)

PESACH SEDER MENU

Traditional Gefilte Fish (p. 3) with Horseradish
Classic Chicken Soup (p. 21) with Fluffiest Matzah Balls (p. 245)
Celery Root Salad (p. 38)
Boiled Chicken from the soup (p. 21)
Sweet Potato and Apple Dish (p. 95)
Pesach Vegetable Casserole (p. 248)
Fresh Peach Whip (p. 264)

PESACH DAY MEAL

Meat Blintzes (p. 246)
Honeyed Roast Duck (p. 48)
Pesach Onion Kugel (p. 249)
Sweet Potatoes with Dried Fruit (p. 250)
Pesach Lemon Pie (p. 261)
Chocolate-Dipped Coconut Bonbons (p. 266)

SHAVUOS MENU

Dairy Moussaka (p. 90)
Pumpkin Soup (Dairy) (p. 25)
Ruchie's Special Pickled Salmon (p. 79)
Layered Pashtida (p. 116)
Stuffed Zucchini Boats (Dairy) (p. 94)
Miri's Fabulous Cheese Cake (p. 225)

ROSH CHODESH MENU

Chicken Livers with Pineapple Tidbits (p. 13)
Pecan Toss Salad (p. 38)
Pumpkin Soup (p. 25)
Potted Roast Beef (p. 56) or Apricot Chicken (p. 44)
Cauliflower Polonnaise (p. 101)
Tri-Colored Pashtida (p. 117)
Challah-Apple Kugel (p. 115)
Shevi's Creme Schnitz (p. 153)

Note:

All recipe measurements are for level (not heaping) spoonfuls.
Cups used in recipes are standard 8-ounce cups.

STANDARD CONVERSIONS

1 ounce................................ 28 grams
1 pound...............................450 grams
1 teaspoon............................5 milliliters
1 tablespoon..........................15 millileters
1 cup butter..........................210 grams
1 inch................................2.5 centimeters
3 teaspoons...........................1 tablespoon
2 tablespoons.........................1 fluid ounce
4 tablespoons.........................¼ cup
16 ounces.............................1 pound

OVEN TEMPERATURE EQUIVALENTS

250°F = 120°C = Gas Mark ½
300°F = 150°C = Gas Mark 2
350°F = 180°C = Gas Mark 3
375°F = 190°C = Gas Mark 4
400°F = 205°C = Gas Mark 5
450°F = 235°C = Gas Mark 7

Ⓟ PARVE

Ⓜ MEAT

Ⓓ DAIRY

APPETIZERS

THE FABULOUS EGG

Cooked eggs contain the highest quality protein of any food. We learn from the Tal-mud, "The egg is better than any other food of the same size." Most of the protein is found in the white of the egg, but most of the minerals and vitamins are in the yolk. The yolk is also a rich source of vitamin D, as well as vitamin B12, magnesium, iron, and calcium. Nutritionists claim that eating eggs can help protect the eyes from cataracts and prevent muscular degeneration.

The American Heart Association recommends that we consume 300 milligrams of cholesterol a day. Since an egg yolk contains about 200 milligrams cholesterol, we should consider cutting down on other high-cholesterol foods so that we can allow ourselves one egg almost every day. Researchers have found that the main thing which raises our cholesterol is the saturated fats and trans fats that are found in margarine, packaged cookies, and other processed nosh rather than the cholesterol inherent in natural foods such as eggs. Most of the fat in eggs is the more healthy, unsaturated type. It is important, however, to cook eggs properly in order to retain as much of their protein, iron, and vitamin B as possible. Raw eggs should be avoided whenever possible because of the risk of salmonella poisoning.

To cook eggs, start by putting them in a pan of cold water. Bring to a boil, then cover them and remove from heat. Let them remain in the hot water for 15 minutes, then drain and cool with running cold water. When they have cooled, they should be put in the refrigerator immediately. They keep refrigerated about 1 week.

Boiled, baked, or fried, eggs are a fabulous contribution to nutrition.

traditional gefilte fish

An old family recipe — your bubby would be proud!

STOCK
1 onion, sliced
2 carrots, sliced
1 tablespoon sugar
1½ teaspoons salt
½ teaspoon pepper
fish bones and head, optional

FISH
2 pounds ground fish (carp, white-
    fish, pike, or a combination)
1–2 large onions, diced
4 eggs
1 tablespoon salt
½ teaspoon pepper
5–6 tablespoons sugar
3–4 tablespoons bread crumbs or
    matzah meal

Fill a large pot ⅓ full with water. Add fish bones and head, onion, carrots, sugar, salt, and pepper. Bring to a boil and cook for 10 minutes.

Prepare gefilte fish: In an electric mixer, combine remaining ingredients. Beat well for about 5 minutes. With wet hands, form mixture into oval-shaped fish balls and gently drop into simmering liquid. Cover and simmer for 1½ hours. Alternatively, fish loaves can be shaped and dropped into boiling water. When fully cooked, cool and slice. Serve with a slice of carrot on top.

Serves 12–14.

glorified gefilte fish

For an alternative to the traditional carrot-topped gefilte fish with horseradish. Dress up your gefilte fish loaf with this scrumptious, tomato-based sauce and bake.

1 loaf frozen gefilte fish

SAUCE
2 large onions, sliced
3 cloves garlic, sliced
1 tablespoon oil

2 tomatoes, chopped
3–4 tablespoons tomato sauce
4 tablespoons water
¼ teaspoon salt
¼ teaspoon pepper

Partly thaw the frozen gefilte fish loaf and cut into ⅓-inch slices. To prepare the sauce, sauté the onions and garlic in oil until onions are tender. Add chopped tomatoes, tomato sauce, water, and seasonings. Simmer until tomatoes are soft. Spread mixture on slices of gefilte fish and bake uncovered in a preheated 350° oven for half an hour. Cover and bake another 20 minutes.

Serves 8.

T I P

When cooking, do not use hot water from the tap. Pipes, especially old ones, are lined with lead which can be leached into the water. Simply use cold water and bring it to a boil.

halibut salad

*A filling salad great for Shabbos lunch or seudah shelishis,
or even a quick weekday lunch.*

4 slices halibut (about 2 pounds) or
   other fish fillet
2 small onions, 1 sliced, 1 diced
½ teaspoon salt, plus a little more,
   to taste
½ green pepper, diced
½ red pepper, diced
1 stalk celery, diced
1 dill pickle, diced

2 hard-boiled eggs, diced
pepper, to taste
½–¾ cup mayonnaise
1 black olive for garnish, optional
1 strip red pepper for garnish,
   optional
5 strips green pepper for garnish,
   optional

Cook fish in a little water with sliced onion and ½ teaspoon salt for about 20 minutes. Let cool. Remove fish and flake it with a fork. Combine flaked fish with diced onion, green and red pepper, celery, pickle, salt and pepper, to taste, and hard-boiled eggs. Stir in mayonnaise until blended. Serve on lettuce leaf or shape fish salad into the form of a fish. Put a black olive for the eye and a strip of red pepper for the mouth. Arrange 5 strips of green pepper halfway down the fish for the fins and tail.

Serves 8–10.

=== TIP ===

*If you find that a fish is too salty, add a cup of
vinegar to cold water and soak the fish in the
mixture to draw out the salt.*

Ⓟ / Ⓓ

tuna empanadas

*A great appetizer choice when making a luncheon, this is a
delightful tuna mixture in a delicious pastry dough.*

DOUGH
½ cup margarine
1 tablespoon sugar
½ teaspoon salt
1 egg
¼ cup cold water
2½ cups flour
2 teaspoons baking powder

FILLING
1 7½-ounce can tuna, drained
1 onion, diced
2 hard-boiled eggs, diced
pinch of pepper
¼ cup water

To make the dough, cream margarine with sugar and salt. Add egg,
water, flour, and baking powder. Make into 10–12 balls. Roll each ball
out on a floured surface into a circle about 4 inches in diameter. Mix
together filling ingredients. Place teaspoonful of filling in the center of
each circle. Moisten edges of dough with water. Fold over and pinch
edges together. Bake on a greased baking sheet at 375° until golden
brown. Serve with chili sauce.

Yields 10–12.

VARIATION

Mushroom or Cheese Empanadas: Fill this excellent dough with
sautéed onions and mushrooms or with cheese mixture from cheese
knishes.

eggplant caviar

A tasty appetizer or spread.

1 medium eggplant, peeled
1 medium red onion
1 medium red pepper
3–4 cloves garlic, chopped

salt and pepper, to taste
4 tablespoons olive oil
2–3 tablespoons techinah, to taste
juice of ½ a lemon

Cut the eggplant, onion, and pepper into bite-sized cubes. Place in a large bowl with garlic. Stir in remaining ingredients. Spread mixture on a greased cookie sheet and bake in 400° oven for 45 minutes, stirring about halfway through, to ensure even roasting. Let cool. Process vegetables in food processor with on-off bursts until it becomes chunky, but not too smooth. To serve as an appetizer, place a heaping tablespoonful on lettuce leaf and top with chopped hard-boiled egg. To serve it as a snack, spread on whole wheat crackers or rye bread.

Serves 6–8.

eggplant roulade

A great and novel appetizer.
Thin long slices of eggplant filled with chopped chicken or meat,
rolled, baked, and topped with a classic mushroom sauce.

1 large eggplant
1 large egg
2 tablespoons cold water
bread crumbs, for dipping
oil, for frying

FILLING
1 pound ground meat
2 eggs, beaten

1 large onion, diced
3–4 tablespoons bread crumbs

MUSHROOM SAUCE
2 tablespoons oil
3 tablespoons flour
1½ cups water
2 tablespoons mushroom soup mix
1 10-ounce can sliced mushrooms,
   drained

Slice eggplant lengthwise into 7–8 very thin, long slices. Sprinkle both sides of each slice with salt and let stand at least 20 minutes. Rinse off salt gently and blot dry. Beat egg with water. Dip each slice of eggplant in egg mixture, and then in bread crumbs. Fry in oil on each side in a large skillet. Combine ground meat for filling with beaten egg, chopped onion, and bread crumbs. Top one end of each eggplant slice with heaping tablespoon of filling mixture and roll up. Place stuffed eggplant rolls on a greased baking pan.

Heat oil for sauce in skillet. Stir in flour. Gradually stir in water, mushroom soup mix, and mushrooms. Bring to a boil, then lower heat and simmer for about 5 minutes. Spoon mushroom sauce over eggplant rolls. Cover and bake eggplant in a preheated 350° oven for 20 minutes, then uncover and continue baking for another 15–20 minutes.

Serves 7.

VARIATION

Instead of dipping slices of eggplant in egg and bread crumbs, place slices on greased baking pan, brush both sides with a little oil, and bake in a 350° oven for 20–25 minutes.

eggplant roulade
with mushroom filling

Similar to the recipe above, here is a pareve eggplant roulade with mushroom filling for those special occasions.

Eggplant slices, prepared as in
    Eggplant Roulade

MUSHROOM FILLING

1 large onion, sliced

½ green or red pepper, sliced

3 tablespoons oil, for frying

1 4-ounce can sliced mushrooms,
    drained

2 eggs, beaten

4 tablespoons bread crumbs

TOMATO SAUCE

1 large onion, sliced

3 tablespoons oil

½ cup tomato sauce

½ teaspoon salt

¼ teaspoon pepper

3 tablespoons sugar

1 cup water

Follow instructions for preparing eggplant slices in previous recipe. Next, sauté onion and pepper in oil until onions are tender. Add mushrooms. Sauté for about 2 more minutes. Stir in eggs and bread crumbs. Continue frying until mixture is firm. Let cool. Place tablespoon of filling on fried eggplant slice. Roll up and place on greased baking sheet. Sauté onion in oil until tender. Combine with remaining sauce ingredients in a pot, stir, and bring to a boil. Spread sauce over eggplant rolls. Bake about 20 minutes until eggplant is tender.

VARIATION

Dairy Roulade: Sprinkle top with grated Muenster cheese, or mix grated Muenster cheese into mushroom filling.

TIP

To keep vegetables green when cooking, remove the lid towards the end of cooking. This will also keep cooked beets red.

meatless moussaka

A superb alternative to the meaty moussaka, this delicious dish is perfect for an appetizer or a luncheon main dish, or even a side dish.

2 medium eggplants, sliced into
   ¼-inch slices
oil, for sprinkling or frying

FILLING
1 large onion, diced
1 small green pepper, diced
2½ cups cooked rice
2 eggs, beaten
salt and pepper, to taste

SAUCE
1 large onion, diced
3 tablespoons oil
1 cup tomato sauce
1 cup water
3 tablespoons sugar
juice of ½ a lemon
½ teaspoon salt

Sprinkle eggplant slices with salt. Let stand 30 minutes. Gently rinse off salt. Lay out slices and sprinkle with vegetable oil. Bake covered for 20 minutes or fry on both sides. To prepare filling, sauté the diced onion and green pepper until tender-crisp and combine with the cooked rice, eggs, salt, and pepper. Mix well. To make sauce, sauté onion until tender. Stir in remaining ingredients.

To assemble: Layer half of the cooked eggplant slices in a greased 9x13-inch baking pan. Place a heaping tablespoonful of rice filling on each slice. Cover with the remaining slices. Pour sauce over eggplant slices. Cover pan and bake at 350° for 20 minutes. Uncover and bake for another 15 minutes, or until tender.

Serves 6–8.

TIP

Onions lose their flavor when frozen, while white garlic becomes stronger.

supreme meatballs
with cranberry sauce

Spice up your meatball dish with a different kind of sauce.

MEATBALLS

2 pounds ground meat or chicken

1 medium onion, diced

⅓ cup water

2 eggs

1 tablespoon onion soup mix,
    optional

½ cup bread crumbs

3 cloves garlic, chopped, or ¼ tea-
    spoon garlic powder

SAUCE

1 16-ounce can cranberry sauce

juice of ½ lemon

1 cup ketchup

2–3 cups water

Mix together ground meat, onion, water, eggs, onion soup mix, bread crumbs, and garlic for meatballs. Combine sauce ingredients in a saucepan and bring to a boil. Shape meat mixture into balls and drop in simmering pot of sauce. Cover and cook for one hour. If the sauce is too thick, add a little more water.

Serves 8–10.

baked chicken wings

An economical and tasty appetizer with a tangy sauce.

1 pound chicken wings

SAUCE
½ cup brown sugar
1 tablespoon soy sauce

1 clove garlic, minced, or ¼ teaspoon garlic powder
paprika, for sprinkling on top

Arrange chicken wings in a shallow baking dish. In a separate bowl, combine brown sugar, soy sauce, and garlic. Spread over chicken wings. Refrigerate several hours or overnight to marinate. Sprinkle with paprika. Bake at 350° for 1½ hours. Baste every half hour.

Serves 6–8.

VARIATION

Sprinkle sesame seeds or chopped nuts over chicken wings halfway through baking.

liver with vegetables

More nutritious, yet ever delicious!
A healthy and unusal variation on classic liver.

1 large onion, sliced
3 tablespoons oil
1 green pepper, cut into short strips
2 stalks celery, sliced on an angle
3 carrots, cut into short, thin sticks
⅔ cup green peas, preferably frozen
1 cup water

¼ teaspoon pepper
salt, to taste
2 tablespoons flour
3–4 tablespoons cold water
8 ounces beef or chicken liver, kashered and cut into 1-inch pieces

Sauté onion in oil until tender. Add pepper, celery, carrots, green peas, and water. Cover and cook for 15–20 minutes until vegetables are tender. Add seasoning. Dissolve flour in cold water and stir into simmering mixture to thicken. Add liver and simmer about 2 minutes.

Serves 6 as an appetizer.

Ⓜ

chicken livers with pineapple tidbits

*The traditional dish with a new twist to refresh your
Shabbos lunch or yom tov menu.*

1 pound chicken livers, kashered
and cut into quarters
3 tablespoons oil, for frying
2 tablespoons soy sauce
1 15-ounce can pineapple tidbits,
with juice from can

¾ cup cold water
⅓ cup slivered almonds
1 tablespoons cornstarch
3 tablespoons vinegar
3 tablespoons brown sugar

Heat oil and sauté chicken livers for about 2 minutes. Add soy sauce,
pineapple tidbits with juice from can, and ½ cup water, and bring to
a boil. In a small bowl, dissolve the cornstarch in remaining ¼ cup of
water and stir into simmering chicken livers until the mixture thickens.
Add slivered almonds, vinegar, and brown sugar, and continue cooking
on low heat for 3–4 minutes.

Serve in patty shells or on a bed of cooked rice.

Serves 6–8.

Ⓜ

chicken fricassee

An old family recipe with a marvelous sweet-and-sour sauce.

1 large onion, sliced
1–2 tablespoons oil
1 cup water, or more
1 cup ketchup

⅔ cup brown sugar, packed, or
white sugar
1½ pounds chicken parts: wings,
necks, and gizzards

Sauté onion in oil until tender. Add water, brown sugar, and ketchup.
Simmer on low heat for a minute. Add chicken parts. Cover, bring to a
boil, and then simmer on low heat for at least an hour until gizzards are
tender. If necessary add more water while cooking. Serve as appetizer
or side dish.

Serves 6.

chicken blintzes

An excellent appetizer, especially when served with mushroom sauce.

BLINTZ BATTER
1¼ cups flour
1½ cups water
½ teaspoon salt
2 eggs
2 tablespoons oil
oil, for frying

FILLING
1 large onion, diced
1 small green pepper, diced
2 tablespoons oil
1 cup sliced mushrooms
1 cup mushroom sauce (see below)
2–2½ cups cooked chicken, cut into
    small pieces

Put batter ingredients in electric mixer bowl or food processor. Mix at a medium or low speed until smooth. Refrigerate at least one hour. When ready to use, stir well. Lightly oil a 7- or 8-inch frying pan and heat. Pour in 2–3 tablespoons of batter, tilting pan quickly from side to side to distribute a thin coating evenly on bottom. Cook over medium-high heat until top of blintz is dry. No need to flip. Turn blintz out of pan and stack on a clean, dry paper towel

For filling, sauté onion and green pepper in oil until onions are tender. Add mushrooms and continue sautéing an additonal 3 minutes. Stir in mushroom sauce and chicken. Put a tablespoon of mixture on each blintz leaf and roll up. Place in a 9x13-inch greased baking pan. Bake at 350° for 20 minutes. Or fry on both sides until golden brown.

Serves 10–12 as an appetizer.

MUSHROOM SAUCE
1 small onion, diced
2 tablespoons oil
1 4–ounce can mushrooms, drained,
    or 1 cup fresh mushrooms, sliced

3 tablespoons flour
1¼ cups water
½ teasoon salt

Sauté 1 onion in oil until tender. Add mushrooms and sauté an additonal few minutes. Push mixture aside and stir in flour until smooth. Slowly add water and salt, stirring, and cook a few minutes until thickened.

chinese chicken blintzes

*Otherwise known as homemade eggrolls —
a special Chinese food appetizer.*

10 blintz leaves

FILLING

1½ cups boneless cooked chicken, diced

salt, to taste

1 teaspoon sugar

2 tablespoons tamari sauce

1 small onion, diced

1 4–ounce can sliced mushrooms, drained

1–2 cups bean sprouts

2 scallions, thinly sliced

1 teaspoon cornstarch

1 egg, beaten, optional

oil, for frying

Prepare blintz leaves (see Chicken Blintzes). Combine chicken with salt, sugar, and tamari sauce. Set aside. Sauté onion until tender. Add mushrooms, bean sprouts, and scallions, and sauté for several minutes. Add chicken mixture to frying pan. Cook on low heat for a few minutes. Push mixture to one side of pan. Stir cornstarch into liquid in empty half of pan until smooth. Combine cornstarch with chicken mixture. Let cool. Place 1–2 tablespoons of mixture in the center of each blintz leaf. Roll, tucking in ends, and seal well. (Use a toothpick or spread on a beaten egg to help seal.) Fry each blintz in oil until golden brown and crisp.

Yields 10 blintzes.

yummy cabbage blintzes

You'll love these tasty blintzes with a tangy taste.

15 blintz leaves

CABBAGE FILLING
1 large onion, sliced
2 tablespoons oil
½ cabbage, chopped (about 3–4 cups)

⅓ cup water
3 tablespoons vinegar
5–6 tablespoons brown or white sugar
1 teaspoon salt

Prepare blintz leaves (see Chicken Blintzes). Sauté onion in oil until tender. Add cabbage and continue to sauté for 10 minutes, stirring occasionally. Add water, vinegar, sugar, and salt. Cover and cook on low heat for 45 minutes, until cabbage is tender and water is absorbed. Fill each blintz leaf with cabbage mixture and roll. Bake in a preheated 350° oven for 20 minutes or fry lightly on both sides until golden brown.

Yield: 15 blintzes.

mock chopped liver

A delicious, crunchy spread that makes an excellent appetizer.

2 large onions, sliced
3–4 tablespoons oil
5 hard-boiled eggs

½ cup walnuts
½ cup canned peas, optional
salt and pepper, to taste

Sauté onion in oil until golden. Let cool. Place sautéed onion, eggs, walnuts, salt and pepper, and peas, if desired, into food processor and process until smooth. Do not over-process. Serve on lettuce leaf, or as a spread.

Serves 6.

VARIATION

With Eggplant: Slice 1 eggplant and sprinkle with salt on both sides. Let rest 30 minutes. Rinse. Fry eggplant in oil on both sides. Sauté 2 large sliced onions in oil until golden. Place fried eggplant, sautéed onions, 3 hard-boiled eggs, salt, and pepper into food processor. Process until smooth. Serve as above.

mock chopped herring

Start your luncheon, dinner, or party right with this decorative, low-calorie, herring-flavored dish.

1 medium eggplant
½ teaspoon plus 2 tablespoons
    olive oil
5 tablespoons cider vinegar
2 tablespoons water
3 slices whole wheat bread

4 hard-boiled eggs
1 medium onion, chopped
2 large apples, peeled and grated
1 tablespoon sugar
salt and pepper, to taste
pinch of ginger

Cut eggplant in half lengthwise. Brush ¼ teaspoon oil on each side and place both halves, cut side down, in 375° oven for about 45 minutes, until tender. Let cool and peel off the skin. Combine vinegar and water in a shallow bowl or pan and soak bread until soft. Squeeze out excess liquid. In food processor, grind the eggplant, squeezed bread, 3 of the hard-boiled eggs, onion, and apples. Add sugar and enough salt to give the mixture the flavor of herring. Add 2 tablespoons oil, ginger, and pepper. Process all the ingredients in a food processor until smooth and spreadable.

To serve, place eggplant mound on lettuce leaf. Mash yolk of remaining hard-boiled egg and sprinkle across half of eggplant mound. Mash the white and sprinkle on remaining top half. Garnish with parsley and wedges of tomato.

Serves 6–8.

TIP

To remove candle wax from tablecloths or carpets, cover it with a paper towel and press with a hot iron. The spot can then be lifted out easily.

avocado-herring spread

A nutritious dish full of omega oils and calcium — but you don't have to be a health-lover to enjoy its taste.

2 avocados, peeled and mashed

3 hard-boiled eggs, chopped

1 16-ounce jar boneless pickled herring pieces, drained

1 small onion, chopped

3–4 tablespoons mayonnaise

1 tablespoon lemon juice

Mix all ingredients together. Serve on lettuce leaf or as a spread.

Yields about 3 cups.

tofu spread

An excellent, low-calorie alternative to cream cheese.

8 ounces tofu, cut into chunks

1 tablespoon soy sauce, scant

3 tablespoons techinah

garlic powder, to taste

1–2 tablespoons lemon juice,
  optional

Combine all ingredients in a bowl. Purée in a food processor or blender or with a blender stick. Use as a spread on pita, bread, or crackers. Can also be spread inside celery sticks.

SOUPS

Though it can at times be challenging, maintaining good relationships with others is of utmost importance, and it takes on even greater significance when we are reminded that sinas chinam — baseless hatred — was the ultimate cause of the destruction of the Beis HaMikdash, as well as of many other tragedies that befell the Jewish people throughout our history.

We must make every effort to keep our friendships and our connections with others strong. But how?

Rav Eliyahu Dessler, the late mashgiach of Ponevezh Yeshivah, had much to say about friendship and about loving our fellowman. In his sefer Michtav Me'Eliyahu (Strive for Truth), he states that in order to love someone you must give to him or her. Giving is the key to loving, and the more you give to another, the more you will come to love him or her. Giving to another also enables one to ward off any animosity or any ill feeling that might have built up.

The act of true chesed, giving, can be performed in various ways. It does not necessarily have to involve an object or a gift. Giving of yourself, of your time, of your energies, or of your know-how in a specific area are all very meaningful ways of giving. Listening, sharing, helping, borrowing, empathizing, giving directions — through all of these acts, especially when the help is sorely needed, you are giving something priceless. No amount of money can buy true friendship. Being patient with another — even when you are under pressure — is a very high level of giving. Phoning someone who is lonely is also a form of giving.

With all of these many ways of giving, you can be sure that the rewards bounce right back — because you will experience for yourself the joy of giving and also increase your capacity for love. As the popular adage goes, "We make a living from what we receive, but we make a life from that which we give."

We can put the homemaker right at the top of the list of selfless givers when we see the many ways she keeps giving. She consistently shows kindness to her spouse, children, and other family members. She prepares and serves endless meals. She expresses love and warmth to her nearest and dearest. With all these forms of chesed, we can truly rejoice in the knowledge that as homemakers, our days and our lives are filled with acts of kindness and giving.

classic chicken soup

Chicken soup's healing power has earned it the title of "Jewish penicillin," and its fabulous flavor — made complete by every woman's special touch — has earned it a time-honored place in every Jewish home on Friday night.

½–¾ of a chicken, cut into eighths or quarters

9 cups water

2 stalks celery, cut into large pieces

1 medium onion, quartered

1 parsley root, cut in half

1 parsnip, cut into thirds

2 medium carrots, cut into chunks

1–2 medium zucchini, cut into chunks

a few sprigs parsley

salt, to taste

turkey neck or soup bones (for a richer flavor), optional

Place all ingredients into a large soup pot. Cover and bring to a boil. Skim off top. Lower heat, cover, and simmer for 1½–2 hours. Let cool slightly and if desired remove chicken and vegetables. Skim fat off top of soup. Can be served as is or with a few small pieces of boneless chicken and vegetables.

Serves 12.

TIP

To absorb the fat from the soup, place a piece of tissue paper or piece of lettuce on the surface of the soup while it is still hot. The fat will cling to the tissue or lettuce leaf. Then remove and discard it.

fresh vegetable soup

This soup is a thick, nutritious, classic blend.
I serve it often for yom tov night meals.

2 large onions, sliced

3 cloves garlic, chopped

3 tablespoons oil

2–3 stalks celery, thinly sliced

3 carrots, sliced

1 parsley root, diced

2 medium zucchini, sliced

8 cups water

2 bay leaves

½ teaspoon dried basil

a few sprigs fresh dill

salt and pepper, to taste

In a large stainless steel soup pot, sauté onions and garlic in oil until tender. Add the celery, carrots, parsley root, and zucchini, and sauté an additional 8 minutes, stirring frequently. Add water, bay leaves, basil, and dill. Bring to a boil, cover, and simmer on low heat for 1 hour. Add salt and pepper 5 minutes before it is finished cooking. If desired purée with hand blender or in a food processor. Return to pot and cook 2–3 more minutes. Remove bay leaves before serving or before blending.

Serves 8–10.

T I P

For a beautiful and elegant soup presentation, try the following: Put a cookie cutter in the center of a soup bowl. Pour a thick, creamy soup in the center of the cutter. Pour a creamy soup of another color (slightly less thick) around the cutter. Carefully lift out the cutter and serve immediately. Alternatively, pour a ladle of one soup into the bowl and then another ladle of a different colored soup beside it. Suggested combinations: pea soup and pumpkin soup; zucchini soup and tomato soup; mushroom soup and carrot soup.

Ⓟ / Ⓓ

cream of mushroom soup

This recipe is made with fresh mushrooms,
which always add a touch of class to your menu.

2 large onions, diced

3 tablespoons oil

½ pound fresh mushrooms, sliced

5 cups water

1 teaspoon salt, or to taste

⅛ teaspoon white pepper

1–2 bay leaves

3 tablespoons flour

2–3 tablespoons cold water

1 tablespoon mushroom soup mix, optional

½ cup pareve or regular cream

In a soup pot sauté onions in oil until transparent. Add mushrooms and cook additional 5 minutes, stirring occasionally. Add water, salt, pepper, and bay leaves. Cover and bring to a boil. Lower heat and simmer for 10 minutes. In a small bowl or cup dissolve the flour in cold water until smooth. Pour into simmering mixture. Add mushroom soup mix if desired. Cook an additional 5–7 minutes. Remove bay leaves and stir in the cream.

Serves 8.

creamy carrot soup

Delightful — and loaded with vitamin A from the carrots.

3 large onions, sliced
3 tablespoons oil
8 carrots, peeled and cut into
   chunks

6–7 cups water
salt and pepper, to taste
1-2 tablespoons pareve onion soup
   mix

Sauté onions in oil until golden. Set aside. Bring carrots and water to a boil. Cover, lower heat, and simmer for 15 minutes. Add sautéed onions and continue cooking another 10–15 minutes until carrots are soft. Add salt and pepper to taste. Add soup mix. Remove from heat and purée with a hand blender until smooth. Serve as is or with croutons or pine nuts.

Serves 8–10.

creamy barley soup with vegetables

Wholesome, nutritious, and delicious!
You'll especially want to make this during cold weather.

⅔ cup pearl barley
10 cups water
2 large onions, diced
3 tablespoons oil
3 carrots, sliced
1 medium or large zucchini, cubed

4 stalks celery with leaves, cut into
   pieces
1½ teaspoons salt
⅓ teaspoon pepper
1 teaspoon basil
2 tablespoons onion soup mix

Put barley into a large soup pot with the water. Bring to a boil, skim off top, cover, lower heat, and simmer for about 1 hour. While the barley is cooking, sauté the onions in oil until tender. Cover pan so that onions will sauté evenly and not burn. To the soup pot, add carrots, zucchini, celery, sautéed onions, salt, pepper, basil, and soup mix. Continue cooking for 30 minutes. Remove from heat and purée with a hand blender or in the food processor.

Serves 12.

Ⓟ / Ⓓ

pumpkin soup

This is a marvelous, satisfying soup, made famous by the Jerusalem Ramada Renaissance Hotel. Perfect for special occasions.

2 large onions, sliced
4 tablespoons oil
7 cups water
1½ pounds pumpkin, cubed
1 medium white potato, cubed
2 medium sweet potatoes, cubed
1 tablespoon pareve chicken soup mix

½ teaspoon salt, or to taste
¼ teaspoon white pepper
½ cup sweet cream or nondairy creamer
3 tablespoons margarine, optional
pine nuts for garnish, optional

In a stainless steel pot sauté onions in oil until golden. Add the water, pumpkin, potato, and sweet potatoes. Bring to a boil. Cover, lower heat, and simmer for about 35 minutes. With a hand blender, purée vegetables until smooth. Add soup mix, salt, and pepper and continue simmering for an additional ten minutes. Stir in cream or non-dairy creamer and remove from heat. Serve sprinkled with pine nuts. For a richer flavor, stir in 3 tablespoons of margarine while hot.

Serves 10.

zucchini soup

Zucchini has very low calorie content,
making this soup a weight-watcher's delight.

3 large onions, sliced

2 tablespoons canola or olive oil

6–8 medium zucchini, cubed

1 medium potato, cubed, optional

1 teaspoon basil

3 cloves garlic, crushed

1 rounded tablespoon pareve
chicken soup mix, optional

7–8 cups water, to cover

salt and pepper, to taste

In a large soup pot, sauté onions in oil until tender. Add zucchini, potato, basil, garlic, soup mix if desired, and water. Bring to a boil. Cover
and lower heat. Simmer gently for 30 minutes. Add salt and pepper
5 minutes before finished cooking. Remove from heat. With a hand
blender, purée vegetables until smooth. Serve hot as is or with croutons
or soup nuts.

Serves 10–12.

VARIATION

Broccoli Soup: Substitute 1 16-ounce package of frozen chopped
broccoli for the zucchini.

split pea soup

Drop some pareve frankfurter pieces into this hearty soup, and you've created an entire meal.

1½ cups split peas, checked
12 cups cold water or soup stock
2 large onions, diced
4 tablespoons oil
3–4 carrots, sliced

2 bay leaves
2 teaspoons salt, or to taste
½ teaspoon pepper
8 pareve frankfurters, cut into 1-inch pieces

Placed the checked split peas and water in a large soup pot. Bring to boil, then simmer for about 1 hour. Sauté onions in oil until tender and add to the simmering soup. Add carrots, bay leaves, salt, and pepper, and cook for an additional hour. Remove bay leaves. Cook or microwave the frankfurters and cut into 1-inch pieces. Serve soup with 3-4 pieces in each bowl of soup.

Serves 12.

creamy red pepper soup

Yes, red pepper soup! Unusual, easy-to-make, and delicious.

4 large onions, sliced
2 tablespoons oil
6 red bell peppers, chopped
5½ cups water

1 rounded tablespoon onion soup mix
salt, to taste
½ teaspoon pepper

Sauté onions in oil until tender. Add peppers and continue sautéeing 10–15 minutes, stirring occasionally. Cover, lower heat, and continue cooking until peppers are softened, an additional 15–20 minutes, stirring occasionally. Add 1½ cups water and purée until smooth with a hand blender or in a food processor. Return mixture to soup pot. Add additional 4 cups water, onion soup mix, salt, and pepper. Cover, bring to a boil, lower heat, and simmer for an additional 25 minutes. Serve with croutons or soup nuts.

Serves 6.

tomato-rice soup

Just right for a cold, wintry day,
this wholesome soup will nourish, satisfy, and soothe.

1 large onion, diced
2 tablespoons oil
2 cups canned tomatoes, or soft
   tomatoes, peeled and chopped
½ cup tomato sauce
5 cups water
1 teaspoon salt, or to taste

¼ teaspoon pepper
1 tablespoon sugar
2 tablespoons flour
⅓ cup cold water
1 cup cooked rice
3 sprigs parsley, chopped, for garnish, optional

Heat oil in a large soup pot and sauté onion until golden. Add tomatoes, tomato sauce, water, salt, pepper, and sugar. Cover and simmer for
25 minutes. Purée with a hand blender or in a food processor. In a small
bowl or a cup, combine flour with ⅓ cup cold water until smooth. Pour
into simmering soup, stirring. Simmer for an additional 2 minutes. Add
cooked rice and cook on low heat 3 more minutes. Ladle into soup
bowls and sprinkle with chopped parsley.

Serves 6.

creamy onion soup

You'd never guess that this delicious soup is so good for you!

4–5 large onions, sliced
4 tablespoons oil
3 tablespoons cornstarch
6 cups water
2 teaspoons sugar

1 teaspoon salt
¼ teaspoon pepper
1 tablespoon onion soup mix,
   optional

Sauté onions in oil until golden brown. Stir in cornstarch until smooth.
Gradually add water, then add sugar, salt, pepper, and soup mix. Bring
to a boil and simmer covered for 20–25 minutes.

Serve 6–8.

Ⓜ / Ⓟ

sweet and sour cabbage soup

*A tangy, hearty traditional soup, made in many Jewish homes
for yom tov, especially Pesach.*

1 large onion, sliced	juice of 1 lemon
3 tablespoons oil	⅓–½ cup brown sugar, or to taste
1 16-ounce bag shredded cabbage	1½ teaspoons salt
1 28-ounce can chopped tomatoes	6 cups water

In a large soup pot sauté sliced onion in oil until tender. Add remaining
ingredients. Bring to a boil and skim off foam. Simmer on low heat for
about 1 hour. Serves 12.

VARIATION

With Meat: Add 1 pound soup meat and bones and cook until meat
is tender. (Trim off fat from meat before cooking.) Substitute 2 cups
tomato juice for the canned tomatoes.

Ⓟ

egg drops

An easy soup accompaniment that perks up plainer soups.

1 large egg	4 tablespoons flour, sifted
¼ teaspoon salt	2 tablespoons cold water
pinch of pepper	

With a fork, beat egg, salt, and pepper. Stir in flour until smooth. Gradually stir in cold water. Pour mixture into soup in a gradual stream from
a tablespoon, holding it fairly high over the pot. Cook for 5 minutes.

(P)

fruit soup

A refreshing soup perfect for a hot summer day,
but well received all year round. Serve chilled.

4 cups assorted fresh fruits
   (peaches, apricots, plums,
   nectarines, grapes, pears,
   blueberries, pitted cherries), cut
   into uniform pieces

6 cups water, plus ½ cup water
¼ cup apple juice concentrate, or to
   taste, or sugar, to taste
3 tablespoons raisins
1½ tablespoons cornstarch

Place fresh fruit, 6 cups water, apple juice, and raisins in a large pot.
Cover and bring to a boil. Reduce heat and simmer for about 20 minutes. Dissolve cornstarch in ½ cup water and pour gradually into simmering fruit 5 minutes before it finishes cooking. Simmer 5 minutes
more. Let cool. Put into containers and refrigerate. Serve with a dab of
sour cream or pareve whipped cream if desired. Can be frozen.

Serves 10.

VARIATION

Omit the cornstarch and instead blend half the soup in a blender and
then mix back into the pot.

T I P

Freeze leftover sauces, soups, and tomato sauce in
ice cube trays. Once frozen, remove the cubes and
store them in a plastic bag. When you need some,
you will be able to defrost exactly
the amount you need.

SALADS

AN APPLE A DAY
KEEPS THE DOCTOR AWAY

For many years, nutritionists felt that it was important to eat apples because of the fiber they contain. Today, however, due to the findings of photochemistry, it has been discovered that apples contain much more than just fiber. Apples, and especially apple peels, contain large amounts of photochemical antioxidants and may be responsible for the prevention of heart disease, cancer, and other diseases.

Many studies regarding this discovery have been conducted at research centers. The studies found that eating 3½ ounces of fresh Red Delicious apples, with their skins, will provide antioxidant activity equaling 1,500 milligrams of vitamin C.

Oxidation in the body can cause cell and tissue damage, resulting in certain diseases. This deterioration, which is caused by excess oxygen, is prevented by antioxidants. Most varieties of apples are beneficial because the photochemicals contained in them not only act as antioxidants, but can also help prevent inflammation, blood clotting, and the spreading of harmful cells. They are also beneficial to the function of the lungs, and inhibit wrinkling of the skin. Moreover, apples contain a lot of pectin, which helps reduce cholesterol.

Other fruits, such as grapes, pears, peaches, and bananas, show even greater antioxidant activity. Among vegetables, garlic shows the highest antioxidant activity, followed by tomatoes and broccoli, which also have high levels of antioxidants.

Yes, an apple or even two a day can keep the doctor away. A convenient snack, they can be taken to work with you and included in the children's lunch boxes. Be sure to wash them before eating and then eat them with the skins on.

crunchy carrot salad

A crunchy, tasty salad with a delicious dressing. Carrots are loaded with vitamin A, which aids in the repair of body tissue and helps maintain smooth, soft skin.

3 stalks celery, diced
5 medium carrots, shredded
1 medium onion, diced
1 red pepper, cut into thin strips
1 yellow pepper, cut into thin strips

DRESSING
¼ cup vinegar, scant
⅓ cup sugar
⅓ cup oil
1 teaspoon salt
½ cup mayonnaise

In a large salad bowl toss together celery, carrots, onion, and peppers. In a small bowl mix together dressing ingredients. Toss together the dressing and the mixed vegetables. Serve slightly chilled.

Yields 1 liter.

spinach salad

This satisfying, unique mix of vegetables and protein adds color and elegance to any table.

8 ounces fresh spinach leaves
1 cup cashews, broken or split
1 cup bean sprouts
½ small red onion, thinly sliced
1–2 hard-boiled eggs, chopped, for
    garnish
a few cherry tomatoes, optional

DRESSING
½ cup oil
⅓ cup sugar
⅓ cup ketchup
¼ cup vinegar
3 cloves garlic, minced

Wash spinach leaves thoroughly in a few changes of water. Check. Tear into pieces. Mix together spinach, cashews, bean sprouts, and onion. Combine ingredients for dressing and mix with spinach salad. Sprinkle chopped eggs on top. If desired, a few cherry tomatoes can be scattered throughout.

Serves 6–8.

red cabbage salad

With cubes of fresh mango. A real favorite!

1 16-ounce bag shredded
  red cabbage
1 mango, cut in ½-inch cubes
1 red onion, diced
⅓ cup slivered almonds
6 tablespoons vinegar

⅓ cup oil
½ teaspoon salt
pepper, to taste
6 tablespoons sugar
1½ tablespoons sesame seeds

In a salad bowl, combine red cabbage, mango, onion, and slivered almonds. In a separate bowl combine vinegar, oil, salt, pepper, and sugar, and pour over the vegetables. Toss together well. Sprinkle with sesame seeds. Serve chilled.

Serves 8.

VARIATIONS

Add a handful of dried cranberries instead of mango.

Add 3 ounces sugared almonds and ¾ cup toasted angel-hair pasta. Omit the mango, sesame seeds, and sliced almonds.

TIP

Everyone enjoys a bargain, but when it comes to buying fresh fruits, use caution. By paying less, you may be buying low-quality fruit, and that affects the fruit's taste and sweetness.

cranberry salad supreme

*Ready for a change of pace? A sweet salad with cranberries and
pecans that will spruce up any menu.*

4 cups fresh cranberries

2 cups sugar

1 24-ounce can pineapple tidbits,
  drained

2 cups seedless grapes, halved

½ cup pecans

1 cup pareve topping, whipped

Process cranberries in food processor with blade. Transfer to a colander
and pour sugar on top. Let stand for about an hour, until they are no
longer dripping. Combine drained cranberries, pineapple, grapes, and
pecans. With an overhand stroke, fold the whipped topping in gently.
Serve individually in attractive dessert dishes or in a crystal bowl.

Serves 8.

bean sprout salad

Healthy, tasty, and easy to make — who can beat this one?

1 cup bean sprouts

2 cucumbers, sliced

1 carrot, thinly sliced

1 green pepper, cut into thin strips

1 red onion, halved and thinly sliced

DRESSING

⅓ cup vinegar

¼ cup oil

⅓ cup sugar

2 teaspoons water

salt, to taste

Toss all ingredients for salad. Combine dressing ingredients and mix
well. Toss together.

Serves 5–6.

eggplant marinade

A novel blend of eggplant and pepper that makes a great side dish for Shabbos meals.

2 eggplants, peeled and cut into
    1-inch cubes
salt, for sprinkling on top
¼ cup olive oil
4 tablespoons vinegar
2–3 tablespoons sugar
3 cloves garlic, chopped

2 bay leaves
¼ cup water
½ red pepper, cut into short strips
1–2 pickles, sliced
generous pinch of pepper
1–2 tablespoons tomato sauce,
    optional

Sprinkle eggplant moderately with salt. Let stand 20 minutes, then rinse lightly to remove salt. Scatter in a greased baking pan. Drizzle oil on top of eggplant pieces. Cover and bake for 45 minutes until eggplant is tender. Let cool. Mix together ingredients for marinade: vinegar, sugar, garlic, bay leaves, and water. Combine with eggplant and remaining ingredients. Serve chilled.

Yields ½ liter.

tangy vegetable salad

This is a real family favorite and crowd pleaser.
We serve it almost every Shabbos.

2 carrots, thinly sliced
2 cucumbers, sliced
1 green pepper, sliced
1 red pepper, sliced
1 yellow pepper, sliced
1 medium onion, sliced

MARINADE
¼ cup vinegar
¼ cup oil
2 tablespoons water
½ cup sugar
1½ teaspoons salt

Combine all vegetables in a large bowl. In a saucepan bring marinade
ingredients to a boil. Pour over vegetables and toss.

chickpea-pasta salad

A meal in itself! Excellent for seudah shelishis.
Chickpeas or garbanzos have twice as much iron
as other legumes and are high in vitamin B.

4 tablespoons wine vinegar
½ teaspoon salt
¼ teaspoon pepper
2 tablespoons sugar
½ teaspoon oregano
4 tablespoons oil

2 cups cooked pasta (bow ties, shells, ziti, etc.)
2 cups canned chickpeas (garbanzo beans)
4 tablespoons parsley, chopped
¼ cup pimento, diced

In a large bowl combine vinegar, salt, pepper, sugar, oregano, and oil.
Add pasta, chickpeas, chopped parsley, and pimento. Refrigerate for a
few hours before serving.

Serves 10.

pecan toss salad

A fantastic vegetable–nut mix with delicious, tangy dressing.

1 12-16 ounce bag shredded lettuce
1 small red onion, thinly sliced
1–1½ cups cherry tomatoes, halved
½ cup sugared pecans

DRESSING

2 tablespoons ketchup

⅓ cup oil
3 tablespoons sugar
3 tablespoons vinegar
2 cloves garlic
2 tablespoons water
salt, to taste

Place lettuce, onion, tomatoes, and pecans in a bowl. In a separate bowl, combine ingredients for dressing and mix well. Toss with salad.

Serves 10.

celery root salad

You'll be surprised at what a delicious salad this is —
nutritious too. Try it!

1 celery root, peeled and shredded
1 large apple, peeled and shredded
½ cup yellow raisins

¼ cup sugar
2 tablespoons lemon juice
¼ teaspoon salt

Combine all ingredients. Mix well. Refrigerate and serve chilled.

Serves 5–6.

vegetable trifle

*A beautiful and appealing way to serve vegetables at a Shabbos
table or a formal get-together.
Use any four or five of the vegetables listed.*

5–6 medium carrots, peeled and
   shredded

2 cups shredded lettuce

1½ cups shredded red cabbage

1 cup shredded white cabbage

1–1½ cups frozen peas, defrosted
   and cooked

1–1½ cups corn niblets, canned, or
   frozen and cooked

3 tomatoes, cut into wedges

DRESSING

1 cup mayonnaise

2 teaspoons lemon juice

¼ teaspoon salt

⅛ teaspoon pepper

½ teaspoon garlic powder

2–3 tablespoons water

GARNISH

cherry tomatoes for garnish, optional

red, green, and yellow peppers, cut
   into strips, optional

2–3 raw mushrooms, halved or
   sliced, optional

In a large salad bowl layer shredded vegetables, corn, peas, and tomato
slices. A combination of four or five of the suggested vegetables can be
used. Combine the dressing ingredients and pour it around the middle
of the top layer. Garnish with cherry tomatoes, strips of red and green
pepper, and slices of raw mushrooms, if desired. Serve chilled.

Serves 8–10.

Ⓟ / Ⓜ

vinaigrette dressing

The classic dressing that gives an added zing to any salad.

¾ cup oil   dash of paprika
2 cloves garlic, minced   3 tablespoons vinegar
1 teaspoon salt   2 tablespoons chopped dill pickle
¼ teaspoon pepper   1 teaspoon chopped parsley

Place all ingredients, except pickle and parsley, into food processor with blade. Run processor for 1–2 minutes. Stir in pickle and parsley. Shake well and refrigerate. Shake again before using.

Yields 1 cup.

VARIATION

Crumble 2 ounces of Roquefort or other blue cheese and add to vinaigrette dressing before using. Shake well.

Ⓟ

homemade croutons

*An excellent recipe for do-it-yourselfers.
Sprinkle on salad for an extra treat.*

8–10 slices of bread, with crust   2 cloves garlic, whole
2 tablespoons oil

Cut bread into small pieces. Place in pan and toast in a 300° oven, stirring frequently, until dry and golden brown. Heat oil in a skillet and add garlic cloves. Add the croutons and sauté until coated with oil. Turn off flame and remove garlic. Place the croutons in plastic containers and refrigerate until ready to use.

POULTRY

LOWERING YOUR CHOLESTEROL INTAKE

It is important for mothers and wives to be familiar with low cholesterol eating. Cholesterol, which clogs the arteries and can cause heart attacks, often starts to build up in early childhood.

Although some of the cholesterol in our bodies is made by the body itself, the rest can be controlled by eating the right foods. Diets high in saturated fats cause cholesterol to build up in the body. Whole grains, fruits and vegetables, and other foods which do not contain saturated fats help to keep cholesterol levels low. Instead of using oil high in saturated fats, use canola, olive, safflower, or corn oils.

In general, one should not buy large bottles of oil because oil can become rancid from standing for long periods of time. Anything with a rancid taste or smell should be discarded immediately. This also applies to commercially bought crackers, cookies, chips, and pastries which contain oil. (A benefit of baking these items yourself is that you can use healthier ingredients.)

Butter and margarine are high in saturated fats, as are coconuts, coconut oil, and palm oils. Animal protein such as meat and chicken is also high in saturated fat. Turkey is lower in saturated fat than other animal protein. For lowering cholestrol and calories, remove the skin of chicken before cooking it. If you plan on roasting the chicken, season it well with garlic, paprika, and a little pepper to replace the taste of the skin.

Another way to lower one's cholesterol level is to eat three cloves of fresh, raw garlic daily. It can be minced or chopped and included in a salad or other prepared dishes. Raw onion is also beneficial in lowering cholesterol.

When sautéing onions, green or red pepper, or mushrooms, use a maximum of 1 tablespoon of oil and sauté on medium heat until the vegetables are tender. Then add a little water, cover, and continue cooking on low heat. Sautéed onions will enhance the flavor of your dish considerably.

Eliminate yellow cheeses and whole milk products with high fat content from your diet. Cut down on condiments like mayonnaise, dressings, and rich sauces. Develop the habit of eating bread without butter or margarine. Instead, spread a spoonful of olive oil on bread or toast, and sprinkle lightly with garlic powder and salt. Add chopped red onions and a slice of tomato for a delicious sandwich.

Another healthier alternative to butter or margarine is avocado, which is delicious as a spread. Avocado contains the good fats, those that benefit the high-density lipo-proteins (HDL) in your blood.

chicken gourmet

This dish has been popular in our family for years. For the chef, it is extraordinarily simple to make; for the crowd, it is delicious.

1 3½-pound chicken, cut into
    quarters
garlic powder, for sprinkling
2 tablespoons ketchup

2 tablespoons honey
½ teaspoon mustard
1 large onion, sliced

Sprinkle chicken lightly with garlic powder and refrigerate a few hours before roasting. Combine ketchup, honey, and mustard and spread over chicken. Place sliced onion in baking pan. Put seasoned chicken on top. Roast uncovered in a preheated 400° oven for 25 minutes. Reduce heat to 350°, cover, and continue roasting for 45–50 minutes.

Serves 4–6.

VARIATION

Cranberry Gourmet Chicken: Use 2 3½-pound chickens. Omit ketchup, mustard, and honey. Instead mix together 1 can of whole cranberries, 2 tablespoons onion soup mix, and 1 tablespoon vinegar and spread over chicken. Cover and roast in a 375° oven for 1¼–1½ hours.

TIP

When planning your menu for an elaborate dinner, try to balance a rich and filling main dish with a light dessert. Some of the lighter desserts are baked apple, fresh fruit, and sherbet. A colorful fruit salad with fruits in season is one of the more popular desserts, especially after a heavy main dish with starchy side dishes.

Ⓜ

apricot chicken

*An easy, flavorful variety of chicken that will fast become a
Shabbos mainstay in your home.*

1 3½-pound chicken, cut into quarters | ½ cup apricot jam
garlic powder, for sprinkling | 2 tablespoons soy sauce
paprika, for sprinkling | 1 teaspoon mustard
1 large onion, thinly sliced | ¼ teaspoon ginger, optional
2 tablespoons oil | 2 tablespoons water

Sprinkle chicken with garlic powder and paprika. Sauté onion in oil
until tender. Add apricot jam, soy sauce, mustard, ginger, and water
and simmer a few minutes. Place chicken in baking pan. Pour sauce
over chicken. Bake in 350° oven until tender, basting a few times, for
about 1½ hours.

Serves 4–6.

Ⓜ

whole roast chicken

Beer gives this chicken an especially tasty flavor.

1 whole chicken | 1 teaspoon paprika
1 medium onion, diced | juice of ½ a lemon
3 cloves garlic, minced | ¾ can of beer
½ teaspoon pepper

Combine onion, garlic, pepper, paprika, and lemon juice and rub inside
and outside whole chicken. Place chicken in roasting pan. Pour beer on
top and into the cavity. Bake in a preheated 350° oven for 1½ hours
until tender.

Serves 4–6.

yom tov chicken

A special dish with all sweet ingredients to enhance your yom tov.
Adapted from a Russian immigrant chef.

2 3½-pound chickens, cut into
    quarters
2 tablespoons oil
4 tablespoons sugar
2 cups water
1 clove garlic, crushed
¼ teaspoon salt

¼ teaspoon pepper
1 tablespoon cornstarch
6–8 prunes, pitted
6 dried apricots
½ cup raisins
1 8-ounce can crushed pineapple,
    drained

Place chicken in a baking pan and bake in a preheated 350° oven for 30 minutes. Meanwhile, in a skillet, heat oil and stir in 2 tablespoons sugar to caramelize. As soon as sugar becomes light brown, stir in water. Add crushed garlic, salt, and pepper. Add another 2 tablespoons of sugar. Bring to a boil. Dissolve cornstarch in a few tablespoons of cold water and stir into simmering mixture. Add dried fruits and pineapple. Cook for 20 minutes. Pour this sauce over prebaked chicken and bake an additional 45–50 minutes until tender.

Serves 8–10.

tangy sesame schnitzel

A delicious new twist on old-fashioned schnitzel.

1½ pounds chicken cutlets (about
 6–8 cutlets)

3 tablespoons apricot jam or honey

3 tablespoons vinegar

1 tablespoon soy sauce

2 tablespoons sesame seeds

Flatten chicken cutlets by pounding on both sides with a mallet. Combine apricot jam, vinegar, soy sauce, and sesame seeds and spread on top of each chicken cutlet. Place on a greased baking sheet and bake in a 400° oven for about 20 minutes.

Serves 6–8.

VARIATION

Nutty Chicken Cutlets: Add ⅔ cup chopped almonds instead of sesame seeds.

honeyed roast duck

This dish makes a festive entrée, with the honey adding a nice touch.

3 cloves garlic, minced

⅓ teaspoon pepper

1 4–5-pound duck

HONEY–APRICOT GLAZE

½ cup apricot jam

2 tablespoons honey

juice of 1 lemon

2 tablespoons orange liqueur or
 brandy

Combine garlic and pepper and rub mixture over raw duck. Refrigerate for 1 hour. Place duck in a roasting pan. Combine ingredients for honey-apricot glaze and pour over duck. Roast in a preheated 375° oven for ½ hour, then lower temperature to 350°. Continue roasting for another 1½–2 hours until tender.

Serves 4–6.

turkey royale

This colorful combination of turkey and vegetables is complemented by a delicious sweet and sour sauce.

1 cup pineapple tidbits, with juice

1 cup ketchup

2 teaspoons mustard

4 tablespoons honey

1 tablespoon soy sauce

½ cup water

1 2½-pound turkey, cut into 1½-inch chunks (breast, thigh, or both)

1 medium green pepper, cut in short strips

1 medium red or yellow pepper, cut in strips

2 tablespoons flour, for thickening, optional

¼ cup cold water, for thickening, optional

In a medium-sized pot, combine pineapple juice, ketchup, mustard, honey, soy sauce, and water. Add turkey, and bring to a boil. Cover, lower heat, and cook for about 1 hour. If necessary, add a little more water. Add green and red peppers and pineapple tidbits, and cook an additional 45 minutes or until turkey is tender. If desired, to thicken sauce, dilute flour in water and stir into simmering mixture. Cook for two minutes until thickened.

Serves 6–8.

VARIATION

Use Chicken instead of turkey. Decrease initial cooking time by ½ hour.

turkey casserole

A great way to use up leftover turkey.

1 medium onion, sliced
2–3 stalks celery, diced
1 small green pepper, thinly sliced
2 tablespoons oil
¾ cup water, plus ¼ cup cold water
½–¾ cup gravy from roast turkey
    (with fat skimmed off), or 1
    tablespoon chicken soup mix

2½ cups cooked turkey or chicken,
    cut into 1-inch cubes
3 cloves garlic, minced, or ¾ tea-
    spoon garlic powder
⅓ teaspoon pepper
3 tablespoons sweet red wine
3 tablespoons whole wheat flour

Sauté onion, celery, and green pepper in oil until onion is golden. Add ¾ cup water, and gravy or soup mix. Bring to a boil, then lower heat. Add turkey or chicken cubes, garlic, pepper, and wine. Dissolve flour in ¼ cup cold water until smooth and stir into the simmering mixture. Cook over low heat for a few minutes, stirring constantly, until sauce thickens.

To serve: Spoon mixture onto a large serving platter. Sprinkle with parsley or coarsely chopped almonds and serve hot over rice or pasta as a main dish or on toast triangles as an appetizer.

T I P

Turkey is the leanest and most economical of all fowl. Because it has such a small amount of fat, it is also more perishable.

frankfurter lunch

Use meat or pareve frankfurters to create a dish that is a big hit, especially with children.

1 medium cabbage, cut into chunks	¼ teaspoon pepper
3 cloves garlic, diced	1 small bay leaf
2 tablespoons oil	½ cup water
3 medium potatoes, cut into 1½-inch cubes, or 8–10 tiny whole potatoes	1 pound miniature frankfurters, whole, or regular frankfurters, cut into thirds
½–¾ teaspoon salt	

Sauté cabbage and garlic in oil for several minutes. Add potatoes, salt, pepper, bay leaf, and water. Cover and simmer on low heat for about 20 minutes, until cabbage and potatoes are tender. Add frankfurters and cook an additional 10–15 minutes. Remove bay leaf before serving.

Serves 4–5.

cantonese chicken with almonds

A delightful Chinese chicken casserole, served with pasta, that makes for an entire meal.

2 cups cooked chicken, cut into cubes	1 teaspoon salt
oil, for frying	½ cup roasted almonds, for garnish
½ cup sliced mushrooms	**SAUCE**
½ cup sliced bamboo shoots	2 cups chicken soup or water
½ cup sliced water chestnuts	2 tablespoons soy sauce
6–8 stalks celery, sliced diagonally	2 tablespoons cornstarch
1 medium onion, diced	

Sauté chicken cubes in oil until golden. Add remaining ingredients and cook until tender crisp, about 15 minutes. Combine soup or water, soy sauce, and cornstarch in a saucepan. Bring to a boil and then simmer until thickened. Combine with chicken and vegetables, then cover and simmer for 6 minutes. Serve hot with noodles and roasted almonds.

Serves 6.

Ⓜ

chop suey

A Chinese dish made with celery, green and red peppers, and mushrooms, served over steamed rice.

1 large onion, sliced
3 tablespoons oil
3 large stalks celery, cut into 1-inch slices (1½ cups)
½ green pepper, cut into short strips
½ red pepper, cut into short strips
1 4-ounce can sliced mushrooms with liquid, or ¼ pound fresh

mushrooms, sliced
2–3 cups cooked chicken breast, cut into 1-inch cubes
¼ teaspoon pepper
2 tablespoons soy sauce
1 tablespoon cornstarch, dissolved in ¼ cup cold water

Sauté onion in oil for 5 minutes. Add celery and green and red pepper and continue sautéeing until tender crisp, about 15 minutes. Add mushrooms with liquid and cook an additional 1–2 minutes. Add chicken cubes, pepper, and soy sauce. Stir in cornstarch dissolved in water. Cook on low fire for an additional 5 minutes, stirring occasionally.

Serves 6.

MEAT

THE JOYS
OF AN ORDERLY LIFE

If you have gone through life thus far without knowing how to be orderly, as countless people have, try learning the following method and see what great satisfaction and contentment there is in living an orderly life. Lack of order leads to frustration, as you frequently search for important items which are just not there when you need them. And neatness is not all there is to order. Orderliness emanates from the mind, and it is much easier to live with an orderly mind than it is to live in a state of mental confusion.

Rav Simchah Zissel Ziv, the mashgiach of Kelm, once visited his son in yeshivah to find out how he was progressing in learning. The mashgiach went directly to his son's room and opened his drawers. When he saw that all of his son's belongings were in complete order, he smiled contentedly, for he knew that his son was learning well.

Do you want to live the rest of your life in relaxed order? If you do, follow this program for an entire week: Each day, before doing anything, think of the next step. Plan ahead for even the simplest, routine household task, such as preparing breakfast. Upon starting, take out all of the utensils you'll need. Then, as soon as you have used them, put them back in their places. Return the cereal box and coffee can to the cabinet and the vegetables to the vegetable bin. When your family is ready to sit down for breakfast, the kitchen counter should be completely clear and clean. A very organized neighbor of mine once told me, "Even if I will need something that I am using five minutes from now, I still put it away as soon as I am finished with it."

Designate a special place for things to be repaired and a certain time for this task. When entering your house, don't just drop your purse and packages on a chair or table near you. Put them immediately in their respective places. Remind yourself of the adage, "A place for everything and everything in its place." If something falls out while you are reaching into a drawer or shelf, straighten it out immediately rather than leaving it for later.

Some good cooks hesitate to try their hand at seemingly complicated recipes because of the large number of ingredients required and the seemingly complicated directions. However, if you keep your kitchen tidy and train yourself to work systematically, even the most complex recipe can be followed with ease.

Remember that you can establish the habit of orderly thinking by "orderly doing" — doing things in a systematic, organized way. Think of the next step with everything you do, and you'll soon discover the joys of an orderly life.

honeyed roast beef with sweet potatoes

In our home, this roast beef was a regular yom tov dish, served on Rosh HaShanah, Sukkos, and Simchas Torah when it is customary to eat sweet foods.

1 4–5 pound beef roast	4–5 carrots, cut into chunks
½ teaspoon pepper	3 sweet potatoes, peeled and sliced
½ teaspoon garlic powder	10–12 pitted prunes, checked
½ teaspoon nutmeg	½ cup honey
1 large onion, sliced	1 cup water

Combine pepper, garlic powder, and nutmeg and rub into meat. Refrigerate 1–2 hours to allow flavors to penetrate. Scatter onion slices in bottom of roasting pan. Place the roast on top of them. Roast in a 375° oven for 45 minutes. Add carrots, sweet potatoes, and prunes. Pour honey on top. Add water to pan and continue roasting at 350° for about 2½–3 hours until meat is tender. Let cool before slicing.

Serves 10–12.

potted roast beef

The top-of-stove method. Classic and delicious.

1 4–5-pound roast (shoulder, brisket, or whole turkey breast)
½ teaspoon garlic powder
½ teaspoon pepper
1 large onion, sliced
3 cloves garlic, minced
2 bay leaves

½ cup water
1 tablespoon vinegar
1 tablespoon brown sugar
½ cup sweet red wine
5–6 potatoes, cubed
3–4 tablespoons ketchup

Combine garlic powder and pepper and rub into roast on all sides. Refrigerate at least 4 hours or overnight. In a Dutch oven sear meat on all
sides. Add onion, garlic, and bay leaves. Add water. Cover and simmer
for 1 hour, turning the meat at regular intervals. If necessary, add a little
more water. Add vinegar, brown sugar, wine, and potatoes. Cover and
continue cooking another hour, turning the meat regularly and checking if there is enough liquid. Add ketchup and cook covered for an
additional hour until tender. Refrigerate for several hours or overnight
before slicing the meat. Skim the fat from the gravy and heat it with the
sliced meat before serving.

Serves 10–12.

TIP

*When making a roast for Pesach — beef or
chicken — add dried apricots and prunes while
roasting for a special flavor and added interest.*

Ⓜ

roast beef
with delicious sweet and sour sauce

Roast beef with a delicious flavor —
you'll get raves every time you serve it.

3 cloves garlic, chopped, or ¾ tea-
    spoon garlic powder
½ teaspoon pepper
1 6-pound roast beef

1 cup brown or white sugar
¾ cup ketchup
½ cup raisins, optional
1½ cups water

Combine garlic and pepper and rub into meat. Let stand 2 hours or refrigerate overnight. Place meat in a roasting pan. Combine sugar, ketchup, raisins, and water and pour over meat. Cover and bake in a preheated 400° oven for 40 minutes. Lower heat to 350° and continue roasting until meat is tender, approximately 3 more hours. Add a little more water while roasting, if necessary. Baste with the sauce 2 or 3 times. Remove cover for last half hour of roasting.

Serves 15.

TIP

To prevent the shrinkage of a roast, wrap it
in aluminum foil first, or cook it slowly on
moderate or low heat.

rolled stuffed tenderloin

Tenderloin beef made into a roulade with a delicious stuffing. A novel way to serve this special cut of beef.

5 pounds beef tenderloin	**STUFFING**
1 large onion, quartered	1 cup bread crumbs
3 carrots, thickly sliced	½ cup flour
1 green pepper, cut into strips	⅓ cup oil
1 cup water	1 teaspoon salt
2 bay leaves	½ teaspoon pepper
½ teaspoon black pepper	¼ teaspoon garlic powder
3–4 cloves garlic	3 tablespoons cold water

Ask your butcher to cut the tenderloin so that it lies flat. Combine all the stuffing ingredients and spread evenly over tenderloin. Roll up meat and tie with heavy white thread. Place in a roasting pan. Place onion, carrots, and green pepper around tenderloin roll. Add water, bay leaves, pepper, and garlic cloves. Cover the roasting pan and roast in a pre-heated 325° oven for 2–3 hours until meat is tender. When done, place meat on a platter surrounded with the vegetables.

Serves 12–14.

(M)

swiss steak with crushed pineapple

A novel way to serve swiss steak.

2 tablespoons flour
½ teaspoon pepper
¼–½ teaspoon garlic powder
1 3-pound shoulder steak, cut into
   1½-inch slices

2 tablespoons oil
1 large onion, sliced
⅔ cup water
2 cups crushed pineapple

Combine flour, garlic powder, and pepper and rub mixture into steaks on all sides. Heat oil in a pot and sauté onion until tender, but not brown. Add steaks and cook for a few minutes on each side. Add water. Cover and cook on low heat for about 1½ hours. Add crushed pineapple, cover, and cook an additional ½ hour, until tender.

Serves 7.

(M)

london broil

The steak in this recipe is marinated in a wine sauce before being broiled to produce an exceptional taste.

2 pounds London broil steak
2 tablespoons olive oil
3 tablespoons wine

2 cloves garlic, minced
generous pinch of pepper
1 tablespoon soy sauce

Score the steak with a fork and put into a shallow pan. Combine the olive oil, wine, garlic, pepper, and soy sauce and pour over steak. Cover and refrigerate for 4 hours or overnight. When ready to cook, place the steak about 2 inches from the heat and broil for 5 minutes. Turn and broil on the other side for 5 minutes. Slice very thin slices across the grain of the meat.

Yields 4–6 servings.

beef tongue with crushed pineapple

*The crushed pineapple gives this high-protein favorite
a distinctive twist, making it a real delicacy.
Serve it on special occasions and holidays.*

1 4-pound beef tongue
3–4 cloves garlic, minced
½–⅔ cup brown sugar, to taste

⅓ cup vinegar
1½ cups crushed pineapple

Boil whole tongue in water for about 3½ hours until tender. Let cool
only slightly and peel while still quite hot for easier peeling. Place cooked
tongue in a baking pan. Combine garlic, brown sugar, and vinegar and
pour over tongue. Spread crushed pineapple on top. Bake in a 350°
oven for about 30 minutes.

Serves 8–10.

VARIATION

With Apricot Sauce: In a saucepan, dissolve 2½ tablespoons cornstarch in ½ cup cold apricot juice. Add ½ cup brown sugar, 6 tablespoons lemon juice, and 2 cups apricot juice. Bring to a boil and
simmer for 3 minutes. Add sliced tongue to mixture. Heat for several
minutes for sauce to penetrate the tongue. If sauce is too thick, add a
few tablespoons water. Serve hot.

M

barbecued brisket

Beef can be a real plus to your protein intake. You can consume as much as one ounce of protein in a quarter pound of roast beef. Try this easy and delicious recipe.

½ teaspoon pepper
3 cloves garlic, minced
1 3–4 pound brisket

1 12-ounce bottle 7-Up
1 cup ketchup

Combine pepper and garlic and rub into brisket. Let stand 2 hours or overnight. Place brisket in a roasting pan. Combine 7-Up and ketchup and pour over roast. Cover and roast in a 350° oven for 2½ –3 hours, until tender. Baste several times while cooking.

Serves 8–10.

M

chinese spare ribs

A popular Chinese dish. Grill these on an outdoor barbeque or broil them in your kitchen oven. Especially good for informal dining.

¼ cup soy sauce
¾ cup water
¼ cup sweet red wine
2 tablespoons brown sugar

2 cloves garlic, minced
4 pounds spare ribs

Mix together soy sauce, water, wine, sugar, and garlic and pour over ribs. Let stand for about an hour, during which time turn the ribs once or twice to marinate all sides. Place the ribs and marinade into roasting pan. Roast in a preheated 375° oven for 1½ hours. Baste frequently, turning the ribs during roasting.

Serves 6–8.

stuffed green peppers with ground meat and rice

A classic dish that is often prepared on holidays like Purim when stuffed dishes are served to represent the hidden miracles in our lives.

6–8 green peppers
1 pound ground meat
2 eggs, beaten
2 tablespoons cold water
1 cup raw rice
¼ teaspoon pepper
3 cloves garlic, minced
1½ cups water

SAUCE
1 large onion, sliced
3 tablespoons oil
1¼ cups tomato sauce
4 tablespoons brown or white sugar
juice of 1 lemon
1¼ cups water
½ cup sliced mushrooms, optional

With a sharp knife cut around the tops of green peppers and carefully remove stems and seeds. Mix together ground meat, eggs, cold water, rice, pepper, and garlic. Stuff peppers with meat mixture and place them upright in a large pot. To prepare sauce, sauté onion in oil. Add tomato sauce, sugar, lemon juice, water, and mushrooms. Bring ingredients to a boil, then lower heat and cook on medium heat for 2 minutes. Pour sauce over stuffed peppers. Add about 1½ cups of water and cook covered for 1½ hours.

spaghetti with meat sauce

*This is a good, practical recipe made with ground meat.
A delicious alternative to meatballs!*

2 large onions, sliced
4 cloves garlic, minced
3 tablespoons oil
1 pound ground meat
3 bay leaves
2 teaspoons chili powder

½ teaspoon black pepper
1 large can tomatoes
1 cup tomato sauce or paste
1 cup water
8 ounces spaghetti, cooked and
　drained

Sauté onions and garlic in oil until onions begin to turn golden. Add ground meat and cook for 10 minutes, stirring constantly. Add bay leaves, chili powder, pepper, tomatoes, tomato sauce or paste, and water. Simmer for 1 hour. If necessary add a little more water. Remove bay leaves before serving. Pour spaghetti sauce over cooked spaghetti and serve warm.

TIP

*For a delicious source of vegetarian protein,
crumble half a pound of tofu into spaghetti
sauce instead of meat.*

roast shoulder of lamb

The unusual combination of ingredients makes this roast lamb a real winner. A great choice when serving company or planning a yom tov meal.

⅓ teaspoon pepper
2 cloves garlic, minced
½ teaspoon paprika
1 3-pound shoulder of lamb

½ cup apricot jam
2 tablespoons vinegar
2 teaspoons prepared mustard, or ½ teaspoon dry mustard

Combine pepper, garlic, and paprika and rub into roast on all sides. Mix together jam, vinegar, and mustard, and spread over roast. Refrigerate for 2 hours or longer. Place roast in a roasting pan. Roast in a preheated 325° oven, uncovered, for 1½ hours, until tender.

Serves 8.

roast shoulder of veal

If you prefer top of the stove cooking, you will enjoy this recipe. Veal is lower in cholesterol and fat than beef and is easier to digest, making it an excellent protein alternative.

3 cloves garlic, minced
¼ teaspoon pepper
½ teaspoon thyme, optional
1 5-pound shoulder of veal

1 large onion, sliced
1 tablespoon oil
2 bay leaves
1½ cups water

Combine garlic, pepper, and thyme and rub into roast. Refrigerate overnight or for several hours. In a stainless steel pot, sauté onion in oil until tender. Add veal roast, cover, and let cook on low heat for about 20–30 minutes. Add bay leaves and water, and bring to a boil. Cover and simmer for about 2½ hours until veal is tender.

Serves 12–14.

stuffed breast of veal

A succulent meat with a tasty stuffing, lighter and easier to digest than beef. I remember this elegant dish being served often in our home when I was growing up.

1 5-pound veal breast
1 teaspoon garlic powder
½ teaspoon pepper
1½ teaspoons paprika

STUFFING
1 large onion, sliced
2 tablespoons oil

1½ cups bread crumbs
3 medium apples, peeled and chopped
1 cup pitted prunes
½ cup raisins
½ teaspoon salt
⅛ teaspoon pepper

Have your butcher cut a pocket in the veal breast. Combine garlic, pepper, and paprika and rub on the outside of the veal. Sauté onion in oil until tender. Remove from heat. Mix together with bread crumbs, chopped apples, prunes, and raisins. Stir in salt and pepper. Stuff mixture into pocket of veal breast. Sew opening together with a needle and a heavy white thread, or close opening with skewers. Place on rack in roasting pan. Cover and roast in a preheated 350° oven for about 2½ hours or until tender.

TIP

Remember to stuff meat just before you put it into the oven. It is not advisable to stuff the meat and refrigerate it until you are ready to roast it, for this allows bacteria to develop.

veal cubes deluxe

An all-around meat dish that everyone will enjoy.

1 large onion, sliced	1½ cups water
1 small green pepper, cut into strips	3 tablespoons sugar, or to taste
2 tablespoons oil	3 cloves garlic, minced
1½ pounds veal, cut into cubes	½ teaspoon oregano
1 cup tomato sauce	generous pinch of pepper

Sauté onion and green pepper in oil until soft. Add veal, tomato sauce, water, sugar, and seasonings. Bring to a boil, cover, and simmer on low heat for about 1½ hours until veal is tender. Serve with spaghetti or brown rice.

Serves 6.

veal amandine

*The almonds enhance the flavor of this tasty casserole
and lend it a gourmet touch.*

1 large onion, thinly sliced	2 tablespoons soy sauce
1 cup thinly sliced celery	½ cup water
2 tablespoons oil	2 cups frozen peas
1½ pounds veal, cut into cubes	⅓ cup slivered almonds

Sauté onions and celery in oil until onions are transparent. Add cubed veal and continue sautéing until onions are golden. Place in a casserole dish. Add soy sauce and water. Cover and bake at 325° for 1–1½ hours until veal cubes are tender. Add peas during the last 20 minutes of cooking time. Sprinkle with almonds for garnish.

Serves 6–8.

veal chow mein

A Chinese food lover's delight

1 medium onion, sliced
1 stalk celery, sliced at an angle
2 tablespoons oil
1 pound veal, cut into thin strips
2 cups water
3 tablespoons soy sauce

salt and pepper, to taste
½ teaspoon garlic powder
2 tablespoons cornstarch
1 4-ounce can sliced mushrooms, with liquid
1½ cups bean sprouts

Sauté onions and celery in oil until onions are tender. Add the veal and sauté on both sides on medium heat until onions are browned. Add water, soy sauce, and seasonings and bring to a boil. Lower heat, cover, and simmer until veal is tender, about 30 minutes. To thicken: Dissolve cornstarch in reserved mushroom liquid and pour, while stirring, into simmering liquid until thickened. Add mushrooms and bean sprouts about 5–10 minutes before finished cooking.

Serves 6.

TIP

Stir-fried Chinese vegetables are popular cooked tender-crisp and not overcooked. This method helps to retain their vitamins and minerals.

classic cholent

Since cooking is forbidden on Shabbos, cholent was innovated by Jews in many countries: a Shabbos noon hot-meal tradition, prepared the day before, then left to cook overnight on a low heat. A large dumpling, called kugel or kishke, was included on top of the cholent. This delicious stew-type dish, which includes meat or chicken, potatoes, barley, and beans, cooks slowly while its flavors blend, spreading a delightful aroma throughout the house. A whole chicken placed on top of the other ingredients will remain intact throughout the night.

2–3 tablespoons sugar
1 tablespoon oil
⅔ cup lima or white navy beans
½ cup barley
1 small onion, diced, optional
1 cup raw rice, optional
2 pounds meat (chuck, flanken, or shoulder), cut into 2 large chunks, or ½–1 whole chicken,

quartered, fat removed
3–4 tablespoons ketchup
soup bones, optional
3 cloves garlic, minced
¼ teaspoon black pepper
7–8 medium potatoes, cut into quarters or eighths
water to cover (about 7 cups)

In a 6–8 quart stainless steel pot, brown sugar in oil, while stirring. As soon as brown, add a cup of water to prevent it from burning. Add the beans to the pot, then barley. If desired, in a separate pot, sauté onion in oil. Combine onion with rice and wrap in cheesecloth or baking paper. Completely immerse bag of rice in water with beans and barley. Add soup bones, if desired, meat, ketchup, and seasonings. Place potatoes on top. Add water to cover all ingredients. Cover and bring the cholent to a boil. Lower heat and simmer for about 1 hour. If necessary, add a little more water. The water should not quite cover the food. Add kishke. Place pot on a covered stove-top (*blech*) over low heat to cook overnight; or place in a 225° oven until lunchtime the next day; or put cholent ingredients into a slow-cooking crockpot, cook on high for about 1½ hours, then cook overnight on low. Do not stir while cooking. To serve, place kishke, meat, and rice on a large platter. Serve potatoes, beans, and barley separately in a large bowl.

VEGETABLE KISHKE

1 large onion, diced	½ teaspoon pepper
2 medium carrots, shredded	½ cup oil
1 teaspoon salt	¼ cup cold water
⅔ cup flour	1 cup bread crumbs

Combine all ingredients and form into a long roll. Wrap in baking paper and place on top of cholent mixture before Shabbos.

pareve vegetarian cholent

*This cholent has all the flavor of meat cholent
yet is strictly vegetarian.*

2 large onions, sliced
3 tablespoons oil
¾ cup pearl barley
2 carrots, cut into large chunks
2–3 stalks celery, cut into 3-inch slices
2–3 medium zucchini, cut into thirds
⅔ cup navy beans

2 sweet potatoes, cubed
4 medium potatoes, cubed
2 teaspoons salt
¼ teaspoon pepper
7–8 cups water, to cover
4 tablespoons ketchup
3 tablespoons honey, optional

In a large stainless steel pot, sauté sliced onions in oil until brown. Add barley. Add remaining vegetables, except potatoes, in layers. Add salt and pepper. Place potatoes on top. Add water to cover and ketchup. Cover and bring to a boil. Lower flame and simmer for at least 1½ hours. Add a little more water, if necessary, to nearly cover potatoes. Put on covered stove-top (*blech*) and let cook slowly overnight.

For a deeper color and more flavor, place 3 tablespoons honey in a skillet with ½ cup of water, and cook 1 minute. Pour into cholent.

VARIATION

Add 1 cup of chickpeas (garbanzo beans) or a block of tofu cut in half.

FISH

THE RAMBAM
ON HEALTHFUL DINING

The Rambam, the famous thirteenth-century Torah commentator, teaches that over-eating is the principal cause of most diseases, a fact which has been corroborated by medical science today. It is important for the homemaker to bear this in mind as she prepares meals for her family. One should eat only when hungry. Even at mealtimes, it is far better not to eat until complete satiety. The ideal way of eating is to consume one-third less than is desired — a difficult feat, particularly in this day and age when food is so plentiful and highly commercialized. The Rambam points out that it is sufficient to eat meat or chicken only once a week. Therefore, housewives can prepare it lichvod Shabbos. Today, however, nutritionists advocate serving meat or chicken three times a week to get an adequate amount of vitamin B12 and protein. Keep in mind that fish, which has many health benefits, can serve as an excellent alternative.

The Rambam maintains that one should avoid drinking during meals since beverages dilute the digestive juices. He also observes that cooked food should not be kept for a long time and reheated repeatedly, for the vitamins are thus destroyed. This is particularly relevant today because of the widespread use of microwave ovens and freezers. The Rambam stresses to go easy on condiments, and to avoid polished and refined grains, such as white rice and white flour, which have very little value. He recommends instead to use whole wheat and other grains in their natural whole state. When baking, whole wheat flour can replace white flour and honey can substitute for refined white sugar.

Introduce whole wheat and whole grains gradually to your family until they become accustomed to it. Use your imagination to cook and bake with whole wheat flour, whole grains, and fresh vegetables and fruits. Your creativity in following the guidelines of the Rambam and of twenty-first century medical science will greatly benefit the health and well-being of your family. The old and healthful way of eating is back in vogue today. Be progressive!

whole stuffed fish

*An elegant way of serving fish. Although the fish is served whole,
the slices are marked and the stuffing can be seen between the slices.
Stuffed whole fish requires longer baking time than unstuffed fish.*

1 3-pound whitefish or carp, whole
1 teaspoon salt
½ teaspoon pepper
½ teaspoon garlic powder
1½ tablespoons oil
juice from ½ lemon
paprika, for sprinkling

VEGETABLE STUFFING
1 large onion, diced
1 small green pepper, diced
1 stalk celery, diced

2 medium carrots, shredded
3 tablespoons oil
3 tablespoons water
1 cup bread crumbs
½ cup mushrooms, sliced, optional
2 eggs, beaten
2 cloves garlic, chopped
1 teaspoon sugar
1 teaspoon salt
generous pinch of pepper

Sprinkle inside and outside of fish with salt, pepper, and garlic powder.
Let stand about 30 minutes for seasonings to penetrate. Brush with oil
and lemon juice and sprinkle with paprika.

To prepare vegetable stuffing: Sauté onion, green pepper, celery, and
carrots in oil for about 5 minutes, stirring. Add water and cover. Lower
the heat and cook an additional 10 minutes until vegetables are tender-
crisp. Remove from heat and combine with remaining ingredients. Stuff
fish with stuffing and place in a large baking pan. Bake in a preheated 350° oven for 45–50 minutes. Cover during second half of baking
time.

Serves 6–8.

TIP

*To avoid the tears onions cause, peel and cut
them under cold running water.*

fish fillet with vegetable stuffing

A unique, colorful, and delicious dish.

2 pounds fish fillets (sole, trout, hake, or cod)
juice of ½ a lemon
3 cloves garlic, minced, or ¾ teaspoon garlic powder
⅔ teaspoon salt
¼ teaspoon pepper
2 tablespoons olive oil

STUFFING
2 tablespoons oil
2 medium onions, sliced
2 large carrots, shredded
2 zucchini, shredded
2 red peppers, diced
1 small green pepper, diced

Combine lemon juice, garlic, salt and pepper and rub into fish fillets on both sides. In a skillet, heat oil, and sauté onions until tender. Add carrots, zucchini, and red and green peppers. Lower heat, cover, and continue to sauté, stirring occasionally until nearly tender, for about 20 minutes. Let cool. Put a heaping tablespoonful of stuffing on top of each fish fillet. Fold the fillet over the filling. Spread about 2 tablespoons olive oil on a baking pan. Place the stuffed fish in the pan and bake in a 400° oven for 20 minutes.

Serves 8.

rolled fillet of sole

This dish of rolled fish fillets stuffed with salmon cubes makes a smashing presentation. Other fish fillets may be used instead of sole.

salt and pepper, to taste
½ teaspoon garlic powder
¼ teaspoon onion powder
1 8-ounce salmon steak,
   cut into cubes

4 large pieces fillet of sole
⅓ cup mayonnaise
4 tablespoons ketchup
chopped parsley, for garnish

Sprinkle salt, pepper, garlic and onion powder on salmon cubes and fish fillets. Let stand about 30 minutes to absorb seasonings. Roll slices of fillet around salmon cubes. Fasten with toothpicks. Place in a greased baking dish. Mix together mayonnaise and ketchup and spread over fish. Bake in a preheated 375° oven for 25 minutes, or until fish flakes easily. Serve sprinkled with chopped parsley.

Serves 4.

baked fish in tomato sauce

"Versatile" is the name of the game. Use this recipe for any and all kinds of fish. A recipe you will want to prepare often.

2 pounds fish fillets (whitefish, trout,
   or pike)
salt, to taste

SAUCE
4 tablespoons ketchup

½ teaspoon mustard
4 tablespoons mayonnaise
3 tablespoons cup water
pinch of garlic powder

Sprinkle fish lightly with salt. Let stand for half an hour. Combine sauce ingredients in a bowl and spread over fish slices. Place in a greased baking pan. Bake in preheated 350° oven for 25–30 minutes.

Serves 8-10.

steamed fish with vegetables

An easy top-of-the-stove recipe.

2 pounds fish (trout, whitefish, or
    pike), sliced
½ teaspoon salt
¾ teaspoon paprika
1 large onion, diced
2 stalks celery, sliced thinly
    at an angle

1 green pepper, sliced
1 clove garlic, minced
2 tablespoons oil
2 medium zucchini, sliced
1 tablespoon soy sauce
3 tablespoons water
½ cup almonds, sliced and blanched

Sprinkle fish on all sides with salt and paprika. Refrigerate or set aside for ½ hour. In a large skillet, sauté onion, celery, green pepper, and garlic in oil until onion is tender. Add zucchini, fish, soy sauce, and water. Cover and cook on low heat for 12–15 minutes. Turn off flame and allow fish to continue steaming for an additional 7 minutes. Serve garnished with sliced almonds on top.

Serves 6.

baked breaded fish cutlets

Baking fish cutlets instead of frying them makes this popular dish healthier and lower in fat content.

2 eggs, beaten
3 tablespoons soy sauce
¼ cup frozen orange juice
    concentrate
1 cup bread crumbs

½ teaspoon paprika
⅓ teaspoon garlic powder
2 pounds fish fillets (pike, sole,
    whitefish, etc.)
3 tablespoons oil

Combine eggs with soy sauce and orange juice. In a separate bowl, season bread crumbs with paprika and garlic powder. Dip fish into egg mixture, then into the bread crumbs. Spread oil on a 9x13-inch baking pan. Place breaded fish in pan. Bake in a preheated 375° oven for 25 minutes.

Serves 8.

ruchie's special pickled salmon

Ruchie Stern served this marvelous dish when I visited her Edison, NJ home. Everyone enjoyed its delicious flavor.

1 2½-pound salmon, cut into 8 slices

PICKLING SAUCE
1 cup vinegar
1½ cups water
¾ cup sugar

3 tablespoons pickling spice
¾ cup ketchup
1 teaspoon salt
¼ teaspoon pepper
1 large Spanish onion, thinly sliced

Combine vinegar, water, sugar, pickling spice, ketchup, salt, and pepper in a medium-sized pot. Bring to a boil. Add salmon, cover, and cook for about 15 minutes. Let cool. With a spatula, transfer salmon to a Pyrex dish. Place thin circles of Spanish onion on top of salmon. Strain the liquid that remains in the pot and pour over fish. Refrigerate until ready to serve.

Serves 8.

Note: Prepare fish 2–3 days in advance to enhance the flavor. Keeps refrigerated for more than a week.

mimi's baked fish patties

An economical, tasty dish made from ground fish.

4 pounds ground fish (carp, pike,
    whitefish, trout, or a combina-
    tion of lean and fat fish)
2 large onions, diced
3 medium potatoes, grated
4 cloves garlic, minced

4 eggs
1 level tablespoon salt
½ teaspoon pepper
2 tablespoons sugar
1–1½ cups bread crumbs

Combine all ingredients and mix well. With wet hands, form into small oval-shaped patties. Place in a well-greased baking pan. Bake in a 375° oven for about 50 minutes, turning once halfway through baking. Serve hot, topped with prepared tomato sauce or mushroom sauce.

Yields 35–40 patties.

TIP

*For a delightful side dish, bake sweet potatoes
together with white potatoes. Slice and peel
both varieties. Sprinkle with salt, paprika, and
oil, and bake for half an hour covered and then
half an hour uncovered.*

salmon fillet with dill sauce

Salmon is high in omega-3 fatty acids,
which have many health benefits.

6 salmon fillets (about 2 pounds)

SAUCE

3 tablespoons mayonnaise

½ teaspoon mustard

1–2 tablespoons pickle juice, optional

1 tablespoon chopped dill or parsley

2 cloves garlic, minced

1 teaspoon paprika

salt and pepper, to taste

Arrange salmon fillets in a greased baking dish. Mix all ingredients for sauce together and spread on top of fillets. Refrigerate for 1 hour. Bake uncovered in preheated 350° oven for 25 minutes.

Serves 6.

salmon and potato bake

*Canned tuna can be substituted for salmon
in this terrific lunch dish.*

2 tablespoons oil

4 tablespoons flour

2½ cups water

¾ teaspoon salt

generous pinch of pepper

1 small onion, diced

¼ green pepper, diced

4 cups thinly sliced raw potatoes

2 8-ounce cans pink or red salmon,
  flaked, or 2 7½-ounce cans tuna

In a skillet, heat oil and stir in flour. Slowly add water, ½ a teaspoon salt, and pepper, stirring until smooth. Add onion and green pepper and simmer for 5 minutes. In a greased baking dish, place alternate layers of sliced potatoes, flaked salmon or tuna with liquid from can, and vegetable sauce. Sprinkle some salt on each layer of potatoes.

Cover and bake in a 350° oven for 20 minutes. Remove cover and bake an additional 25 minutes until potatoes are soft.

Serves 6.

TIP

*To add color to mashed potatoes, mix them
with some cooked, colored vegetables — try
spinach to make them green, or cooked carrots
to make a golden color.*

Ⓟ / Ⓓ

tuna chow mein

Serve over noodles or rice for a light lunch or supper. Fry it with whole wheat noodles for an extra-nutritious dish.

1 onion, diced
2 stalks celery, diced
½ green pepper, diced
1 tablespoon oil
1–2 7½-ounce cans tuna, drained
½ cup water

1 can cream of mushroom soup
  (dairy or pareve)
pinch of pepper
¾ cup cashew nuts
⅔ cup or 1 can chow mein noodles

Sauté onion, celery, and green pepper until onions are tender. Transfer to a bowl and stir in tuna, water, mushroom soup, pepper, and cashew nuts. Pour mixture into a 1½-liter baking dish or casserole. Sprinkle chow mein noodles on top. Bake in a 350° oven for 30 minutes.

Serves 6–8.

TIP

To make a substitute for patty shells, cut off crusts from sliced white bread. Brush with salted margarine and press into muffin tins. Toast in moderate oven.

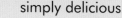

tuna-vegetable pie

A delightful, savory pie with a cheesy crust topping.

1 7½-ounce can tuna, drained
1 small onion, diced
½ small green pepper, diced
1 cup mixed vegetables (cooked, canned, or frozen)
1 tablespoon lemon juice
pinch of pepper
1 tablespoon flour
¾ cup tomato juice

CHEESE CRUST TOPPING
1 egg
½ cup milk or water
¼ cup oil
1 cup flour
1 teaspoon baking powder
1 tablespoon sugar
½ teaspoon salt
½ cup shredded cheddar or mozzarella cheese

Combine tuna, onion, green pepper, vegetables, lemon juice, and pepper. Dissolve flour in tomato juice and add to tuna-vegetable mixture. Place mixture in a greased casserole dish or a round 8-inch greased baking pan. To make topping: Beat egg. Add milk or water, oil, flour, baking powder, sugar, and salt. Stir in grated cheese. Spoon over top of tuna-vegetable mixture. Bake in a 400° oven for 25–30 minutes.

Serves 6.

TIP

Cheese and dishes made with cheese should be cooked very slowly. Fast cooking and high temperatures toughen the cheese and make it rubbery.

VEGETABLES

STUDIES SHOW THAT
COLOR COUNTS

All the years that I cooked for my family, I tried to be aware of the food value of the various ingredients that I put together for each meal. I knew that vitamin A was in carrots and sweet potatoes, that vitamin D was in milk products, and that meat and poultry excelled in the B vitamins. It was important to me to put out a nutritious meal.

Recent research has found that food value can be determined by color as well as by vitamins. Putting the right-colored foods together in planning a nutritious meal for your family can achieve the goal of a nutritious, well-balanced meal.

Red fruits and vegetables, such as strawberries, raspberries, tomatoes, red peppers, and beets, are beneficial to your blood vessels and an aid against certain serious illnesses. Bing cherries are known to alleviate arthritis pain as well as reduce inflammation.

Green fruits and vegetables, such as kiwi, broccoli, peas, lettuce, asparagus, and zucchini, have been found to slow down age-related loss of vision and reduce the risk of asthma and heart disease, particularly in men.

Purple and blue fruits such as blueberries, grapes, and plums contain loads of antioxidants and phytochemicals which help to prevent loss of memory as well as infections.

Yellow and orange fruits and vegetables, such as sweet potatoes, carrots, pumpkin, red lentils, cantaloupes, and apricots, are also beneficial to your eyesight and general health and well-being, reducing the growth of cataracts, strokes, lung cancer, and type 2 diabetes.

White and brown thin skinned vegetables such as mushrooms, cauliflower, garlic, potatoes, and onions have marked nutritional benefits against heart disease as well as asthma.

The Food and Drug Administration recommends that one should consume five to nine servings of fruits and vegetables every day, and other researchers advise eating as many as nine to eleven servings of fruits and vegetables each day for better health. Half a cup of fruit or vegetables is considered one serving. By eating, for example, 2½ cups of vegetables and 2 cups of fruit each day, you can assure yourself a healthful, nourishing daily intake of fruits and vegetables, a marked boon to robust health.

vegetarian "meatballs"

This take-off of classic meatballs is an excellent alternative for vegetarians. The balls can be baked or fried before being boiled in tomato sauce.

2 large onions, diced
1 stalk celery, diced
3 carrots, shredded
1 cup mushrooms, sliced
3 tablespoons oil
3 eggs
⅔ cup matzah meal
1 cup canned peas
½ teaspoon salt
¼ teaspoon pepper

⅓ cup walnuts, optional

TOMATO SAUCE
1 large onion, diced
3 tablespoons oil
1 cup tomato sauce or paste
2 cups water
2 tablespoons vinegar
¼ cup sugar
¼ teaspoon salt
1 teaspoon oregano

Sauté onions, celery, carrots, and mushrooms in oil for about 15 minutes. Let cool and process in a food processor. Stir in eggs, matzah meal, peas, salt, pepper, and walnuts. Let stand for about 10 minutes for the mixture to become firm. Roll into small balls. Place on a greased baking sheet and bake in a preheated 350° oven for 20 minutes, or fry in oil until browned. In a pot, sauté onion for tomato sauce. Add rest of sauce ingredients and bring to a boil. Drop in vegetarian balls and cook for 20 minutes. Serve over rice or pasta.

Serves 6.

TIP

Deep-fry carrot sticks instead of potatoes for a delicious and nutritious vegetable fry.

spinach soufflé

A light and fluffy quiche imitation, without the hassle of a crust.

1 large onion, sliced
2 tablespoons oil
2 tablespoons flour
1 cup milk or water
1½ cups fresh or frozen chopped
 spinach, cooked and drained

⅔ teaspoon salt
¼ teaspoon pepper
½ cup grated cheddar or mozzarella
 cheese
1 cup cottage cheese, optional
4 eggs, well beaten

Sauté onion in oil until tender. Stir in flour until smooth. Add milk, spinach, salt, and pepper. Cook for 2 minutes. Remove from heat and stir in grated cheese, cottage cheese, and beaten eggs. Pour into a well-greased 7-inch ring mold pan or a 1-quart casserole dish. Place pan in a larger pan of hot water. Bake uncovered in a preheated 350° oven for 50-60 minutes.

Serves 6.

red cabbage delish

A delightful, hot, red cabbage dish with a sweet and sour tang.

1 large onion, sliced
3 tablespoons oil
1 bag shredded red cabbage
4 tablespoons vinegar

½ cup sweet red wine, or water
1 teaspoon salt
⅓ teaspoon pepper
5 tablespoons jam, or white or
 brown sugar

Sauté onion in oil until tender. Add cabbage and sauté an additional 10 minutes, stirring occasionally. Add remaining ingredients, cover, and simmer on low heat for ½ hour or until cabbage is tender.

Serves 8–10.

onion quiche

This onion quiche is an absolute favorite in my family. Prepare it in advance, freeze it, and serve warm after a fast for a meal that everyone will enjoy. Recent research has found that onions retain their nutritional value even after they are cooked, unlike other vegetables which lose many of their nutrients in boiling.

CRUST
1½ cups flour
½ teaspoon salt
½ cup shortening
3 tablespoons cold water

FILLING
3 large onions, sliced

3 tablespoons oil
5–6 eggs, beaten
1½ cups milk
1 teaspoon salt
⅛ teaspoon pepper
1 cup shredded cheddar or mozzarella cheese

Mix together the flour, salt, and shortening until mixture resembles peas. Sprinkle in water and mix into a dough. Refrigerate for 1 hour. Roll out dough or pat it into the bottom and up the sides of a 9-inch round baking pan.

For filling, sauté onions in oil until golden, about 20 minutes. Remove from heat and let cool slightly. Combine with the remaining filling ingredients. Pour filling into crust and bake in a preheated 350° oven for about 40 minutes.

Serves 8.

VARIATION

Tuna Quiche: Omit the sliced onions and salt. Combine a 7½-ounce can of tuna, drained, with 2 tablespoons mayonnaise and one small chopped onion. Combine with rest of filling ingredients, and pour into prepared crust. Bake as above.

dairy moussaka

A delightful appetizer or even a luncheon main dish.

1 large eggplants, unpeeled and sliced
½ teaspoon salt
2 eggs, beaten
2 tablespoons cold water
flour, for dipping
oil, for frying

CHEESE FILLING

4 ounces cheddar cheese, shredded
8 ounces cottage cheese
3 ounces feta cheese, crumbled
2 eggs, beaten
⅓ cup bread crumbs
2 garlic cloves, minced

1 teaspoon chopped parsley,
   optional

TOMATO SAUCE

1½ cups tomato sauce
2 tomatoes, diced
1 large onion, sliced
1¼ cups water
2 tablespoons oil
1 teaspoon garlic powder
2–3 tablespoons sugar
1 teaspoon salt, scant
½ teaspoon pepper

Sprinkle eggplant slices with salt and let stand ½ hour. Rinse off lightly. Combine eggs with water and dip each slice in mixture. Then dip in flour. Fry slices in oil on each side until golden. To prepare filling, mix together cheddar cheese, cottage cheese, feta cheese, beaten egg, bread crumbs, garlic, and parsley. Put a layer of eggplant slices in a greased baking pan. Place a tablespoonful of filling on each slice and cover with a second slice. Sauté sliced onion in oil until tender. Add remaining ingredients for sauce and simmer 2 minutes. Pour over eggplant slices. Cover with aluminum foil and bake at 350° for 15 minutes. Remove cover and bake another 20 minutes.

Serves 8.

---TIP---

To prepare a pot of cooked barley, simply combine 1 cup barley with 2½ cups water. Add salt and 1 tablespoon of oil, cover, and cook for approximately 1½ hours.

mushroom barley casserole

A filling, delicious, and nutritious casserole. Barley is one of the easiest grains to digest and is rich in calcium, iron, and vitamin B.

3 cups water
1 cup barley
1¼ teaspoons salt, or to taste
½ pound fresh mushrooms, sliced, or 1 10-ounce can mushrooms, drained

2 large onions, diced
½ green pepper, diced
4 tablespoons oil
generous pinch of black pepper
¼ teaspoon thyme, optional

In a large pot, bring water and barley to a boil, together with 1 teaspoon salt. Lower heat and simmer for 1½ hours, stirring occasionally. Meanwhile, in a skillet, sauté mushrooms, diced onion, and green pepper in oil until onions are golden, stirring occasionally. Add remaining salt, black pepper, and thyme and simmer over low heat for 5 minutes. Combine with the cooked, drained barley. Put the mixture in a 1½-quart greased casserole or baking dish and bake uncovered in a 350° oven for 30 minutes.

Serves 8.

cheesy baked potato

*Baked potatoes themselves are not fattening or high in calories.
What makes the dish a dieter's nightmare is embellishing it with
butter, margarine, rich sour cream, and other high-calorie toppings.
The recipe that follows is a satisfying, nutritious side dish with only
100 calories per serving.*

2 medium potatoes
1 cup low-fat (½% or 1%) white
    cheese
¼ cup chopped scallions

salt, to taste
¼ teaspoon garlic powder, optional
2 tablespoons cheddar or mozza-
    rella cheese, grated

Bake potatoes in a preheated 400° oven for 45 minutes, or microwave
potatoes on high for 7–10 minutes. Cut in half lengthwise. Scoop out
each half and mash them all together with the cream cheese, scallions,
salt, and garlic powder. Refill shells and sprinkle grated cheese on top.
Return potatoes to oven and heat until cheese is melted. Serve immediately.

Serves 2.

stuffed green peppers
with cheese and rice

Halved green peppers filled with rice and a tasty tomato sauce. An excellent recipe, especially for milchig fare. Prepare it during the nine days or any time you want to serve dairy to family or guests.

4 light green peppers, cut in half
    lengthwise
1 large onion, diced
4 tablespoons oil
1⅓ cups raw rice
3 cups water
1 teaspoon salt, or to taste

8 ounces cheddar or mozzarella
    cheese, grated

TOMATO SAUCE
1 cup tomato sauce
1¼ cups water
¼ cup vinegar or lemon juice
⅓ cup sugar

Brush green pepper halves with oil and place on a greased baking dish. Bake in a preheated 350° oven for 20 minutes to soften. Set aside.

Sauté onion in 2 tablespoons oil until tender. Stir in rice and continue sautéing for a few minutes. Add water and salt, and cover and cook until water is absorbed, about 20 minutes. Meanwhile prepare tomato sauce: Combine ingredients in a saucepan and bring mixture to a boil. Lower heat and simmer for a few minutes.

When rice is ready, stir in remaining 2 tablespoons of oil and grated cheese. Stuff green pepper halves with rice mixture and place in a greased baking dish. Pour tomato sauce over peppers. Bake in a preheated 350° oven for 35–40 minutes.

Serves 6–8.

VARIATION

For pareve stuffed peppers, omit the grated cheese.

broccoli soufflé

A delicious pareve side dish that can be made with or without the cornflake crust. Broccoli is a high-fiber vegetable that is a good source of both potassium and vitamin A.

CRUST
1 cup cornflakes, crushed
½ cup flour
2 tablespoons margarine
¼ teaspoon baking soda

FILLING
2 tablespoons oil
1½ tablespoons flour

½ cup water
⅓ cup mayonnaise
1 small onion, diced
4 eggs, beaten well
salt and pepper, to taste
1 10-ounce package frozen
    chopped broccoli, cooked and
    drained

Combine all crust ingredients and spread in a greased 8- or 9-inch round baking pan. Heat oil in a skillet and stir in flour until smooth. Gradually add water and cook on a low heat for 1 minute, stirring until thickened. Remove from heat and combine with mayonnaise, onion, eggs, salt, and pepper. Stir well. Fold in the cooked chopped broccoli. Pour broccoli mixture into crust. Bake in a 350° oven for 50 minutes.

Serves 6–8.

TIP

Leafy vegetables and broccoli lose half of their vitamins when stored in the refrigerator for more than 5 days.

broccoli bake supreme

A rich, dairy version of broccoli soufflé.

1 large onion, thinly sliced
2 tablespoons oil
1 tablespoon flour
½ cup water
8 slices American cheese, cut into
    1-inch strips

1 10-ounce package frozen broccoli,
    cooked until tender
3 eggs, beaten well
½ cup bread crumbs
2–3 tablespoons olive oil

Sauté onion in oil until tender. Stir in flour until smooth. Stir in water. Add cheese and cook on low heat until cheese is melted. Remove from heat. Add cooked broccoli and then stir in beaten eggs. Pour mixture into greased casserole dish or baking pan. Sprinkle bread crumbs on top. With a tablespoon, drizzle oil on top. Bake in a preheated 350° oven for 40 minutes.

eggplant parmesan

This Italian dish is a nice change from the usual carbohydrate-filled dairy main dishes.

1 eggplant, peeled and sliced into
    ⅓-inch slices
salt, for sprinkling
1 cup flour
3 tablespoons oil

1 large onion, diced
¾ cup tomato sauce or paste
¾ cup water
¼ teaspoon pepper
1 cup shredded Parmesan cheese

Sprinkle eggplant slices with salt and let rest about 20 minutes. Rinse. Dredge in flour. Fry in oil on both sides. Drain on absorbent paper towels. Sauté onion in remaining oil until tender. Add tomato sauce or paste, water, and pepper. In a greased baking pan arrange the sautéed eggplant and tomato mixture in alternate layers. Sprinkle cheese on top of each layer of tomato sauce. Bake in a preheated 350° oven for 25 minutes.

Serves 6–8.

italian eggplant "pizzas"

This recipe substitutes eggplant rounds for pizza crust, with marvelous results. A low-calorie, kid-friendly dish.

1 large, elongated eggplant, sliced
   into ½-inch rounds (8–10 slices)
⅓ cup oil
1 cup bread crumbs
1 teaspoon salt

⅛ teaspoon pepper
½ teaspoon garlic powder
2 teaspoons oregano
½ cup pizza or marinara sauce
6–8 slices mozzarella cheese

Brush both sides of each eggplant slice with oil. Combine bread crumbs with salt, pepper, garlic powder, and 1 teaspoon oregano. Dip eggplant slices into seasoned bread crumbs and place on a large greased baking pan. Cover and bake in a preheated 375° oven for about 40 minutes, until tender. Remove pan from oven and spread a spoonful of pizza sauce on each slice. Place a slice of cheese on top and spread it with pizza sauce. Sprinkle top with oregano. Return to oven and bake an additional 10 minutes until cheese is melted.

Yields 8–10 servings.

stir-fried chinese vegetables with noodles

Stir-frying is a quick method of cooking that preserves the vegetables' nutrients. Make this dish in a wok or a skillet.

2 cups fine noodles, raw
¼ cup oil
3 stalks celery, cut into 1-inch slices
1 large green pepper, cut into short strips
1 medium onion, diced

1 4-ounce can sliced mushrooms, with liquid
3 tablespoons soy sauce
½ cup water
2 cups bean sprouts

In a large skillet or wok, stir-fry noodles in oil until golden brown. Add celery, green pepper, and diced onion. Cook for 2–3 minutes. Add mushrooms, soy sauce, water, and bean sprouts. Cover and simmer for 15 minutes, until vegetables are tender-crisp. If necessary, add a few more tablespoons water.

low-calorie oven vegetables

Try these tasty veggies baked in the oven.

1½ cups cauliflower, florets, fresh or frozen
1½ cups sliced zucchini
3–4 tablespoons low-calorie garlic or vinaigrette dressing

¾ cup bread crumbs
2 tablespoons grated Muenster cheese
paprika, optional

Blanch cauliflower in boiling water for about 3 minutes. Drain. Combine with zucchini. Add dressing and mix well to coat vegetables. Roll vegetables in bread crumbs to cover and sprinkle with grated cheese and lightly with paprika, if desired. Place on a well-greased 11x17-inch cookie sheet. Stir a few times while baking. Bake in preheated 400° oven for about 15 minutes or until golden brown.

Serves 6.

broiled vegetable cutlets

These delightful vegetable cutlets are broiled instead of fried, making them lower in calories and easier to digest. A good way to get children to eat their vegetables.

2 large onions, diced
4 tablespoons oil
2 cans mixed vegetables, drained
2 eggs, beaten

salt and pepper, to taste
2 cloves garlic, diced, or ⅓ teaspoon
    garlic powder
⅔–¾ cup matzah meal

Sauté onions in oil until tender. Meanwhile, place drained vegetables in a food processor with blade and process slightly with on-off pulse. Do not purée. (Cooked frozen or fresh vegetables can be used instead of canned.) In a bowl, combine eggs, sautéed onions, slightly processed vegetables, salt, pepper, and garlic. Stir in matzah meal. Let stand for about 10 minutes. Form into patties and place on a greased baking pan. Broil for 15–20 minutes until brown. Turn patties over and brown on the other side. Serve with tomato sauce or mushroom sauce.

Yields about 8 nice-sized patties.

= T I P =

Zucchini or squash cut into large chunks will enhance the flavor of almost any soup. Easy to digest and low in calories!

cauliflower polonaise

The word polonaise indicates the use of bread crumbs. A unique side dish that will add a flash of white to your table.

1 10-ounce package frozen cauli-
    flower, or 1 head cauliflower,
    separated into florets
3 tablespoons oil
½ cup bread crumbs

1 teaspoon lemon juice
salt and pepper, to taste
1 tablespoon parsley, chopped
½ teaspoon paprika, optional

Cook cauliflower in a small amount of water until just tender but not too soft. In a skillet, heat oil and stir in bread crumbs, sautéeing for a few minutes. In a bowl combine the cooked, drained cauliflower with lemon juice, salt, pepper, and paprika if desired. Add to the bread crumbs in the pan and add parsley. Sauté together for 3-4 minutes.

Serves 8.

zucchini stir-fry

Your whole family will enjoy this easy-to-make Chinese style stir-fry with zucchini and mushrooms.

1 large onion, sliced
2 tablespoons oil
2 medium green pepper, cut into
    strips
½ red pepper, cut into short strips
3 medium zucchini, julienned (cut
    into 1-inch-long strips)

5 fresh mushrooms, sliced, or 1
    4-ounce can sliced mushrooms,
    drained
3 tablespoons soy sauce
½ teaspoon garlic powder
1 teaspoon salt, to taste
pinch of pepper

Stir-fry sliced onions in oil on medium heat for 5 minutes. Add green and red pepper, zucchini, and mushrooms and stir fry until tender-crisp, about 15 minutes, stirring frequently. Add soy sauce, garlic powder, salt, and pepper and stir-fry an additional 3–5 minutes.

zucchini creole

Marvelous and versatile, serve this tomatoey dish as a topping for rice,
kasha, or couscous, or as an embellishment for baked fish or chicken.

1 large onion, sliced
1 small green pepper, cut into thin
   strips
1 stalk celery, thinly sliced
3 tablespoons oil
2 medium tomatoes, cut into cubes
2–4 tablespoons tomato sauce
1 cup water

1 teaspoon salt, or to taste
generous pinch of pepper
2 teaspoons sugar, or to taste
2–3 cloves garlic, diced
3 medium zucchini, cut into cubes
1 4-ounce can mushrooms, drained,
   optional

Sauté onion and green pepper in oil until tender-crisp. Add celery, tomatoes, tomato sauce, water, seasonings, zucchini, and mushrooms.
Cover and simmer for about 25 minutes, stirring occasionally.

soufflé à la zucchini

A light, fluffy side dish to go with any meal.

2 pounds zucchini, peeled and
   thickly sliced
3 eggs, well beaten
2 tablespoons flour
2 tablespoons mushroom soup mix,
   optional
2 tablespoons oil

1 teaspoon salt
¼ teaspoon pepper
3 tablespoons matzah meal
1 handful of crushed potato chips
   or Bisli, for sprinkling on top,
   optional

Cook zucchini in a small amount of water until tender, about 20 minutes. Drain well. Transfer to a bowl and mash. Add eggs, flour, mushroom soup mix, oil, salt, pepper, and matzah meal. Pour mixture into a
well-greased casserole or loaf pan. Bake in a preheated 350° oven for 30
minutes. Sprinkle crushed potato chips or Bisli on top, if desired. Cut
into squares or slices and serve hot.

*The following recipes are traditional simanim
for Rosh HaShanah*

ⓟ

honeyed carrots

*"Mehren," meaning "many," is the Yiddish word for carrots. By
eating carrots, we express our hope for numerous merits on the
upcoming Day of Judgment. The round slices of the carrots also
represent completeness and our hope for a complete year.*

2 pounds carrots, peeled and sliced
    into circles
4 tablespoons oil
4 tablespoons honey
½–1 teaspoon salt

1 teaspoon cinnamon
⅓–½ cup orange juice
½ cup raisins
⅔ cup crushed pineapple, optional

Cook carrots over medium-high flame for 2–3 minutes, stirring occasionally. Add oil, honey, salt, and cinnamon. Cover and continue
steaming on a very low heat for half an hour. Add orange juice, raisins,
and pineapple and cook an additional 15–20 minutes.

Serves 6–8.

ⓟ

cubed crookneck squash

*Crookneck squash is called "k'ra" in Hebrew, which means "to tear."
When we eat this squash, we pray that all evil decrees be torn up
and discarded.*

4 cups cubed crookneck squash

2 cups sugar

Cut squash into 1½-inch cubes. Put into a pot with sugar. Start cooking
on medium heat for a few minutes, then on low heat for about 1 hour.
Let cool. Serve cold or at room temperature.

(P)

tiny spinach patties

"Silka," the Aramaic word for beets or spinach, has the root meaning
"to remove" and alludes to the hope that our enemies be removed.

4 cups fresh chopped spinach, or
    frozen spinach, defrosted
1 medium onion, diced
1 cup bread crumbs, or ¾ cup
    matzah meal

2 large eggs, well beaten
1 teaspoon salt
¼ teaspoon garlic powder
1 teaspoon sugar
oil, for frying

Mix all the ingredients together well. Form into very small patties and
fry in hot oil on both sides, until golden.

(P)

black-eyed peas

Black-eyed peas are known as "rubia," meaning "many" in
Aramaic. When we eat the rubia, we ask Hashem to give us many
merits on this Day of Judgment.

½ cup sugar
2 tablespoons oil
water, for cooking peas

1 cup dried black-eyed peas, soaked
    in hot water overnight

Brown sugar in oil on low heat, stirring occasionally. When brown, add
a little water to stop the browning process. Add black-eyed peas and
just enough water just to cover. Cook covered on low heat for 1½–2
hours, until soft. Serve cold.

KUGELS

LET'S KEEP IT NUTRITIOUS

Since the homemaker has the responsibility of preparing meals for her family, she should try to be aware of the various new findings in nutrition as well as the individual needs of her family members. Today's nutritionists have compiled much information regarding the benefits of natural foods — such as fresh fruits and vegetables, whole grains, and soya products — that emphasize the vitamin, mineral, and fiber content of each food.

There are over forty important vitamins, minerals, and enzymes that we need in our diet. A small percentage is stored by the body, but most must be replaced constantly through the food we eat. Vitamin C, which is found in fruits, especially citrus, and vitamin D, the sunshine vitamin, which can also be obtained from dairy products, must be replenished daily.

Millions of dollars are spent annually on vitamin supplements, and although they are helpful, especially for people with certain vitamin deficiencies, there is very little which can replace the vitamins contained in fresh or even frozen and canned foods, as long as the foods are prepared properly.

A word about stress in today's fast-paced society: It is important to create a stress-free environment, especially around mealtimes. Stress is harmful to one's diet for a number of reasons. First, it negatively affects one's digestive system, preventing your body from properly absorbing nutrients even from healthy foods. Second, it can actually destroy existing vitamins in your body. And finally, stressful lifestyles generally mean that people do not properly prepare or eat healthy meals.

We have access today to much information and guidance in purchasing and preparing most varieties of foods. It is certainly worthwhile to keep yourself informed.

potato kugel with sesame topping

Made with cooked potatoes and sautéed onion —
absolutely delicious.

8 medium potatoes, cooked and
    mashed
2 large onions, sliced
4 tablespoons oil
1 cup flour
4 eggs
¼ cup vegetable oil

1½ teaspoon salt
¼ teaspoon pepper
1 egg beaten with 1 tablespoon
    water
3 tablespoons sesame seeds,
    optional

Sauté onions in oil until tender. Add them to mashed potatoes. Beat the eggs well and stir them into the mashed potato mixture. Add oil, salt and pepper, and flour. Pour into a well-greased 9x13 inch baking pan. Brush top with beaten egg. Sprinkle top with sesame seeds, if desired. Bake in a preheated 350° oven for 45–50 minutes.

apple kugel

This kugel is prepared like a cake, but has a kugel–like consistency.
Serve as an accompaniment to a roast beef or chicken dinner,
and add raisins or pecans to give it added zest.

4 eggs, beaten
1 cup sugar
2 teaspoons cinnamon
½ cup oil
1 cup flour

1 teaspoon baking powder
6 tart apples, peeled and sliced
½ cup raisins, optional
⅓ cup chopped pecans, optional

Combine eggs, sugar, cinnamon, and oil. Stir in flour and baking powder. Fold in sliced apples, raisins, and nuts. Pour into a well-greased 9x13-inch pan and bake in a preheated 350° oven for 45–50 minutes.

(p)

leah's sweet potato kugel

It's truly superb — just like its name!

5 cups canned, or cooked and
    mashed, sweet potatoes
2 eggs
4 tablespoons oil
½ cup brown sugar or honey

1 teaspoon cinnamon
½ teaspoon salt
⅓ cup flour or matzah meal
grated rind and juice of ½ lemon

Mix all ingredients together and pour into 9x13-inch baking pan lined
with baking paper. Bake in a preheated 350° oven for about 1 hour.
Serve hot as a side dish for chicken or turkey.

Serves 10–12.

VARIATION

Make individual kugelettes by baking in muffin tins, filled ⅔ of the
way. Decrease baking time to 40 minutes.

(p)

batya's crunchy-top sweet potato kugel

Everyone is sure to ask for seconds of this luscious, nut-topped kugel.

6 medium sweet potatoes, peeled
    and cut into chunks
3 eggs, beaten
½ cup Coffee Rich
½ cup brown sugar, packed
2 tablespoons flour
1 teaspoon vanilla

TOPPING
½ cup margarine
1 cup coarsely chopped almonds or
    pecans
½ cup brown sugar, packed
1 cup flour

Boil sweet potatoes in water until soft. Remove from water, mash, and
combine with eggs, Coffee Rich, brown sugar, vanilla, and flour. Place
in a greased 9x13-inch baking pan. For the topping, melt margarine and
combine with chopped nuts, brown sugar, and flour. Spread over sweet
potatoes. Bake in a preheated 350° oven for about 50 minutes.

Serves 10–12.

noodle kugel and kugelettes

A rich and tasty version of the classic lukshen kugel. Because it can be served at room temperature, it makes an excellent side dish for Shabbos lunch.

1 8-ounce package medium
    noodles, cooked and drained
3 eggs
⅓ cup oil
½ cup brown sugar, packed
1 teaspoon cinnamon
1 cup white raisins

½ teaspoon salt
1½ cups orange juice
grated rind and juice of ½ lemon
oil, for kuglettes
brown sugar, for kugelettes
pecan halves, for kugelettes

With electric mixer, beat together the eggs, oil, brown sugar, cinnamon, and salt. Stir in raisins, orange juice, and lemon juice and rind. Stir in cooked noodles. Pour mixture into a 9x13-inch greased baking pan and bake in a preheated 350° oven for 1 hour. Serves 12–14.

For kugelettes, pour 1 teaspoon of oil, 1 teaspoon of brown sugar, and 1–2 pecan halves into each section of a well-greased muffin tin. Spoon noodle mixture on top of nuts. Bake in a preheated 350° oven for 30 minutes.

yerushalmi kugel

All the ingredients in this kugel — including the noodles — are cooked together in one pot. This is a time-honored recipe that will always be enjoyed, especially when served at a Kiddush on Shabbos.

½ cup oil
½ cup sugar plus 4 tablespoons
6 cups water
1½ teaspoons salt

1 teaspoon black pepper
1 pound fine noodles
3 eggs, beaten

Heat oil and ½ cup sugar, stirring occasionally. As soon as the mixture starts to boil and turns dark brown, remove from fire. Add water slowly. Keep the lid over the pot since the oil splatters. Return to heat and bring to a boil. Add salt, pepper, noodles, eggs, and additional 4 tablespoons of sugar. Cook exactly 6 minutes. Remove pot from stove and let it cool for about 1 hour. Keep covered. Line the bottom of 3 small loaf pans with parchment paper (cut to size) and transfer noodle mixture. Bake in a preheated 350° oven for 1 hour. Kugel should have a dry appearance and a rich brown color when done.

Yields 18 slices.

=== T I P ===

When baking cake, cookies, or kugel, line the pan with baking paper instead of greasing it.

vegetable kugel and kugelettes

Versatile, colorful, and always delicious.

2 large onions, diced	1¼ cups flour
4 tablespoons oil	1 level teaspoon baking powder
4 eggs, beaten	1 teaspoon salt
5 medium zucchini, shredded	¼ teaspoon pepper
2 carrots, shredded	½ cup bread crumbs

Sauté 1 onion in 1 tablespoon of oil until tender. In a bowl, beat eggs, and stir in second diced onion, 3 tablespoons oil, zucchini, carrots, flour, baking powder, salt, pepper, and sautéed onion. Stir well. Pour mixture into well-greased muffin tins and sprinkle with bread crumbs. Bake in a preheated 350° oven for 25–30 minutes.

Alternatively, for regular vegetable kugel, pour entire mixture into a greased 9x13-inch baking pan, sprinkle with bread crumbs, and bake in a preheated 350° oven for about 50 minutes.

Yields 12–14 kugelettes or 12–14 servings.

rice pudding with crushed pineapple

Crushed pineapple lends a sweet and fruity touch to this unique kugel.

3 cups cooked rice	1 cup crushed pineapple
3 eggs	⅓ cup sugar
¼ cup oil	⅓ cup raisins
3 tablespoons instant vanilla pudding mix	1 teaspoon cinnamon
	⅓ teaspoon salt

Combine all ingredients. Pour into a greased 9x13-inch baking pan and bake in a preheated 350° oven for 45 minutes. Remove from oven and let stand 10 minutes. Cut into squares. Serve hot.

Serves 10–12.

tsippie's mushroom pie

I love serving this dish for melaveh malkah, but its versatility allows it to be served anytime, in a pareve, milchig, or fleishig meal.

3 large onions, sliced
⅓ cup oil
1 4-ounce can sliced mushrooms, drained, or 1½ cups fresh sliced mushrooms
3 eggs, beaten
½ cup flour

¼ teaspoon pepper
1 teaspoon salt
1 1-pound package puff pastry dough

GLAZE
1 egg yolk, mixed with 1 tablespoon water

Sauté onions in oil until golden. Remove from heat, let cool, and stir in remaining ingredients. Divide puff pastry dough in two. Roll out half of dough into a rectangle and place onto a greased 9x13-inch baking pan. Spread filling on top. Roll out remaining dough and cut into 1-inch-wide strips. Arrange in lattice top by placing strips over the filling about 1 inch apart, first vertically, then horizontally. Combine egg yolk with water to make glaze and brush over top layer of dough. Bake in a pre-heated 425° oven for 20 minutes. Reduce heat to 350° and continue baking for an additional 15–20 minutes or until golden brown.

Serves 12.

TIP

When using puff pastry dough, start baking at 425° for 15–20 minutes. Then reduce to 350° and bake until golden. Starting the baking at high heat will yield a flakier crust.

cabbage kugel

The cabbage in this kugel replaces the starchy noodles, rice, or potatoes — the old-time kugel regulars — to make a healthful, delicious dish.

2 large onions, sliced
3 tablespoons oil
1 16-ounce bag shredded white
    cabbage
½ cup flour

1 teaspoon salt
½ teaspoon pepper
2 tablespoons mushroom soup mix
4 eggs, beaten

Sauté onions in oil until tender. Stir in cabbage, and continue satéing for 10 minutes. Stir in flour, salt, pepper, and mushroom soup mix. Remove from heat, let cool slightly, and stir in the eggs. Pour mixture into a greased 9x13-inch baking pan. Bake in a preheated 350° oven for 1 hour.

Yields 12–14 squares.

special zucchini kugel

This kugel makes a hit every time.

6 medium zucchini, peeled and sliced
1 large onion, sliced
3 tablespoons oil
1 4-ounce can sliced mushrooms,
    drained
⅓ cup mayonnaise

1 tablespoon onion soup mix
½ cup bread crumbs or matzah meal
1 teaspoon salt
¼ teaspoon pepper
4 eggs, beaten

Cook zucchini in a small amount of water for about 10 minutes. Drain liquid. Chop in a food processor with blade with on-off bursts (not too fine). Sauté onion in oil until tender. Combine with the remaining ingredients, including zucchini. Pour into a well-greased casserole or baking pan and bake in a preheated 350° oven for 45 minutes, until lightly brown on top.

Serves 12.

zahavale's onion kugel

A unique and delicious recipe, and very simple to prepare.

3 eggs
½ cup oil
1 teaspoon salt

generous pinch of pepper
3 large onions, diced
1 cup flour

Beat eggs until fluffy. Combine with remaining ingredients. Pour into a well-greased loaf pan. Bake in a 350°oven for 1 hour.

Serves 8.

ahuva's zucchini top kugel

*Two colorful vegetable layers make for an eye-catching,
appetizing side dish.*

BOTTOM LAYER
2 eggs
4 medium carrots, finely shredded
3 large potatoes, shredded
1 large onion, diced, sautéed in 2
    tablespoons oil
½ cup oil
1 cup flour
1½ teaspoons salt
¼ teaspoon pepper

TOP LAYER
4 eggs, well beaten
½ teaspoon salt
pepper, to taste
2 tablespoons mayonnaise
2 pounds zucchini (6–7 medium
    zucchini), thinly sliced in a food
    processor
1 tablespoon mushroom soup mix,
    optional

To prepare bottom layer: Beat eggs well. Stir in carrots, potatoes, sauteed onions, oil, flour, salt, and pepper. Pour mixture into a greased 9x13-inch baking pan. Mix together ingredients for the top layer and spread on top. Bake in a preheated 350° oven for 45–50 minutes.

Serves 12.

challah-apple kugel

Also known as "bread pudding." Use up leftover challah with this delicious, sweet recipe. A real winner!

1 whole challah, thickly sliced
4 eggs
1 cup white sugar, or ¾ cup brown sugar and 4 tablespoons white sugar
¾ cup oil

½ teaspoon salt
1 package instant vanilla pudding
4 large apples, sliced
⅔ cup raisins
1 teaspoon cinnamon

Remove crust from challah and soak in hot water. Let cool and squeeze out water. In a mixing bowl beat eggs until fluffy. Add ¾ cup sugar, oil, salt, and vanilla pudding and mix until smooth. Stir in the challah, sliced apples, and raisins. Place in a 9x12-inch greased baking pan. Combine cinnamon with remaining ¼ cup sugar and sprinkle on top. Bake at 350° for 1 hour.

Serves 12.

VARIATIONS

Coconut Bread Pudding: Add 1 cup coconut.

Fruit Bread Pudding: Stir in 1 cup of chopped dates or raisins.

Nut Bread Pudding: Add ½–⅔ cup coarsely chopped nuts.

Caramel Bread Pudding: Caramelize ½ cup sugar, stirring it in a pan over medium heat until brown. Pour a little of the water from the soaked challah over the caramelized sugar in the pan as you stir it. Add to kugel.

Banana Bread Pudding: Add 1 cup mashed banana to mixture. Omit the apples.

Individual Kugelettes: Spoon mixture into greased muffin tins. Bake 35–40 minutes.

layered pashtida

Pashtida is a Sephardi quiche, with or without a crust. This recipe has a rich, dairy topping which complements the mushrooms and onions underneath.

CRUST
2 cups flour
1½ teaspoons baking powder
½ cup margarine
3 ounces white cheese

VEGETABLE FILLING
3 medium onions, diced
3 tablespoons oil
1 8-ounce can mushrooms, drained,
or 1½ cups fresh mushrooms, sliced
½ teaspoon salt
¼ teaspoon pepper

CHEESE TOPPING
4 eggs, well beaten
2 tablespoons mushroom soup mix
1½ cups sour cream
¼ teaspoon salt

To make crust: mix together flour, baking powder, margarine, and white cheese. Pat dough into a 9x13-inch greased baking pan. Bake in a 350° oven for 12 minutes.

Next, sauté onions in oil until nearly tender. Add mushrooms and continue sautéeing for several minutes, stirring occasionally. Add salt and pepper. Let cool slightly and spread over prebaked crust. Beat eggs for topping until fluffy. Stir in mushroom soup mix, sour cream, and salt. Spread over first mixture and bake in a preheated 350° oven for 30–40 minutes.

Serves 10–12.

TIP

When entertaining a large crowd, you can do the cooking yourself, but hire someone to serve and clean up afterwards.

tri-colored pashtida

Three layers of bright, eye-catching colors make a very festive side dish. Prepare this for yom tov or for any special occasion.

3 medium potatoes, cut into chunks

4 medium sweet potatoes, or 6 carrots, cut into chunks

10 ounces chopped spinach

8 ounces cheddar or mozzarella cheese, shredded

8 ounces white cheese

8 ounces sour cream

1 cup flour

1 teaspoon salt

¼ teaspoon black pepper

½ cup milk

4 eggs, beaten

Boil potatoes in water until soft. Drain well and mash. In another pot, boil the sweet potatoes or carrots until soft. Drain and mash. Cook spinach in a small amount of water. Drain well. Combine remaining ingredients in a large bowl. Combine ⅓ of mixture with mashed white potatoes. Spread on bottom of greased 12x14-inch baking pan to make a white layer. Bake in a preheated 350° oven for 8 minutes. Combine ½ of remaining cheese mixture with mashed carrots or sweet potatoes. Spread on top of white layer to make an orange layer. Bake for an additional 8 minutes. Combine remaining cheese mixture with cooked spinach to make a green layer and spread on top of orange layer. Return to oven and bake for 45 minutes. Turn off oven. Leave pashtida in oven for 5 more minutes.

Serves 10–12.

TIP

If you are short one egg for baking, substitute one teaspoon of cornstarch. You will never know the difference.

cheese and bell pepper pashtida

*A unique combination of sautéed peppers and cheeses that adds
a nice touch to a dairy meal.*

CRUST
2½ cups flour
½ cup margarine
½ teaspoon salt
⅔ cup water

FILLING
4 large bell peppers, assorted
    colors, cut into strips

2 large onions, sliced
3 tablespoons oil
1 cup sour cream or plain yogurt
1 egg, beaten
3 ounces cheddar cheese, shredded
3 ounces feta cheese, shredded
salt and pepper, to taste

Combine crust ingredients and mix well to form a dough. Roll out ¾ of dough and spread in a greased or lined 9x13-inch baking pan. Sauté peppers and onions in oil for about 10 minutes. Stir occasionally. Lower heat, cover, and continue to steam until tender. If necessary, add a few tablespoons of water to prevent burning. Let cool. Add sour cream, egg, cheddar cheese, feta cheese, salt, and pepper. Mix together well and spread evenly on dough. Roll out remaining ¼ piece of dough and make lattice top as follows: Cut dough into ¼-inch strips. Place strips over filling, about 1 inch apart, first vertically, then horizontally. Bake in a 350° oven for 45 minutes.

cauliflower latkes

A delicious, light alternative to potato latkes.

1 head cauliflower, cut into florets,
    or 1 bag frozen cauliflower
3 eggs, beaten

½ cup flour or matzah meal
salt and pepper, to taste
oil, for frying

Boil cauliflower florets in salted water until tender. Process in a food processor with blade or blender. Stir in eggs and flour or matzah meal. Fry in hot oil on both sides until golden brown.

Yields 12–15 latkes.

vegetable latkes

A colorful, healthy addition to your dinner table.

2 medium carrots
2 medium zucchini
1 medium potato
1 medium onion
small piece of celery root, optional

3 large eggs
½ cup flour
½ teaspoon garlic powder
salt and pepper, to taste
oil, for frying

Cut up vegetables and process in a food processor until fine. Beat eggs until light and fluffy. Add processed vegetables, flour, garlic powder, salt, and pepper. Let stand 10 minutes. Fry latkes in hot oil until golden brown.

Yields 12–15 latkes.

apple-nut latkes

Something different for a side dish or dessert,
with an apple-cinnamon flavor.

3 eggs, beaten
2 tablespoons sugar, or to taste
½ teaspoon cinnamon
⅓–½ cup chopped nuts

6 tablespoons white or whole wheat flour
2–3 apples, peeled and shredded
oil, for frying

Mix together eggs, sugar, cinnamon, chopped nuts, and flour. Add apples. Drop by tablespoonful into hot oil and fry on both sides until golden brown. Place on paper towel to absorb excess oil. Garnish with chopped parsley if desired.

Yields 12–14 latkes.

PASTA, RICE & TÓFU

tofu sandwiches

Quick, easy, and fun, this is a meal that your kids will love and a great on-the-go snack.

1 8-ounce block firm tofu
2 tablespoons soy sauce
3 tablespoons nutritional yeast
3 tablespoons cornmeal
1 teaspoon salt

¾ teaspoon black pepper
½ teaspoon garlic powder
1 tablespoon oil
1 large onion sliced, optional

Preheat oven to 425°. Cut tofu into ¼-inch slices, allowing two slices per sandwich. Lay slices on a plate and cover both sides evenly with soy sauce. Mix dry ingredients in a small bowl. Dip tofu pieces into mixture and lay pieces on a well-greased baking sheet. Bake for 10 minutes. Turn pieces over. If desired, put slices of onion on baked tofu and bake an additional 6 minutes. Serve on whole wheat bread, hot or cold, with ketchup, mustard, or mayonnaise.

TIP

For a delicious peanut butter and jelly sandwich, brown the sandwich in oil and sprinkle with powdered sugar. Cut in half.

CHALLAH & BREAD

THE MITZVAH OF
SEPARATING CHALLAH

The mitzvah of separating challah is one of the three fundamental mitzvos that the Jewish woman is obligated to perform.

A woman has a special zechus, merit, when performing this mitzvah, a zechus which benefits her entire family. At the time that the three angels came to tell Avraham Avinu that Sarah Imeinu would have a son, she was in her tent in the midst of kneading the challah (Bereishis 18:8, Rashi). The separation of challah, hafrashas challah, brought blessing into the home of Sarah Imeinu and will bring blessings into your home as well.

Our Sages tell us that the mitzvah of hafrashas challah is performed to rectify the sin of Chava in connection with the Tree of Knowledge, and that performing the mitzvah of hafrashas challah eases pain in childbirth. Therefore, some women specifically bake challah during the months before giving birth. Some women also try to perform the mitzvah of hafrashas challah during the Ten Days of Repentance, in order to acquire a clean slate before Yom Kippur.

With what quantity of dough is hafrashas challah performed?

According to the ruling of the Chazon Ish, a berachah is said while separating challah when using a minimum of 5½ pounds of flour. When baking with less than that amount, the challah is separated without a berachah. According to Rav Chaim Na'eh, the amount of flour that obligates us in a berachah is 2 pounds and 13 ounces. The piece of dough that is separated should weigh about an ounce.

The berachah is said just prior to the separation of the dough. The dough should be burnt in the oven either before or after baking the bread, but not while the bread is baking. If it is not feasible to burn it, it should be wrapped in a piece of paper, put aside to be discarded, and then declared — either verbally or by thought — as challah.

Here are some challah and bread recipes that were tested with success. I hope they will encourage you to take part in this important mitzvah.

challah

There is nothing like the aroma of challah baking to bring warmth and comfort into your home. Be sure to separate challah from the dough in accordance with halachah.

4 eggs

1 cup oil

1 cup sugar

5 pounds (17 cups) flour

5 cups water

5 tablespoons dry yeast

2½ level tablespoons salt

3 tablespoons honey

GLAZE

1 egg yolk, beaten with 1 teaspoon water

Place eggs, oil, sugar, 5 cups flour, and 3 cups water in electric mixer. Mix on low speed for a few minutes until combined. Add 7 cups flour and yeast and mix again. Add remaining flour, 2 cups water, and salt. Mix until combined. Add honey and knead into a soft dough. Smear top with a little oil. Turn dough over. Cover and let rise in a warm place, free from drafts, for about 2 hours, until double in bulk. Punch down. Divide into 8 pieces for 8 challahs. Divide each piece into 3 sections and braid. Cover and let rise for 1½ hours. Brush tops with glaze. Bake in a preheated 375° oven for 30–35 minutes.

Yields 8 challahs.

VARIATION

Honey Challah: Instead of 1 cup of sugar, use ¾ cup of honey in addition to the 3 tablespoons indicated in the recipe.

TIP

If you want your dough to rise faster, put it into the oven, covered, with only the pilot light on. It well then rise within an hour.

onion kichel

A fantastic sugar-free nosh.

4 cups flour
1 teaspoon baking powder
2 large onions, grated
½ cup oil

2 eggs
1 teaspoon salt
¼ teaspoon pepper
2 tablespoons water

Combine flour and baking powder in a mixing bowl. Stir in remaining ingredients to make a dough. Knead dough for 2 minutes. Divide into 3 parts. Roll each part into ¼ inch thickness. Transfer rolled-out dough to baking sheet lined with baking paper. Cut into squares. Bake in a 375° oven for 20–25 minutes.

Yields 18 kichel

DESSERTS

SERVING FOOD
WITH EYE APPEAL

Besides preparing food that is tasty and nutritious, it is important to serve it in an appealing fashion. Serving food with eye-appeal increases its festivity. Just as you would dress in harmony, making sure that everything matches, so too, your table and all that it encompasses should be elegant and inviting.

Dishes that are attractively served not only stimulate your appetite, but add interest and flair to the meal. The color of the food is important. Try to vary and comple-ment the colors of the various foods on the table. If you are serving, say, zucchini, string beans, spinach, or another green vegetable, complement it with a contrasting color. The orange of carrots, sweet potatoes, or pumpkin is a good choice to go with those green garden vegetables. The white of cauliflower is another fitting contrast.

Garnishes always add appeal to the food you serve. Even greens as simple as parsley, en-dive, or fresh mint can favorably enhance the appearance of whatever you are serving. Place a lemon slice with the edge dipped in paprika alongside baked or broiled fish.

Be creative with a special knife to cut zigzag melon slices, potatoes, and carrots — or use a melon baller on watermelon and cantaloupe for a melon ball cock-tail. Garnish desserts with mounds of whipped cream, chocolate curls, sprinkles, or maraschino cherries.

Finally, make sure that your table is neatly set and inviting. Choose a color scheme, blending or contrasting your colored napkins with the tablecloth. Your guests are guaranteed to be impressed! Include the proper serving pieces to go with the platters or bowls from which the food is being served.

When preparing for a family simchah, it is important to remember that you, as the hostess, add much to the event. The hachnasas orchim — the warmth, welcoming spirit, and enthusiasm that you radiate — will be remembered by the guests long after they have forgotten the decorative table settings.

apple cobbler

The apricot jam gives this apple cobbler a special flavor. Enjoy!

FILLING

6 apples, peeled and sliced

2–3 heaping tablespoons apricot
   jam

CRUMB TOPPING

½ cup margarine

1 cup flour

¾ cup sugar

1½ packets vanilla sugar

Mix apples with apricot jam and spread in a greased, round 9-inch baking pan. Mix together topping ingredients and sprinkle on top of apples. Bake in a preheated 350° oven for 40–45 minutes.

Serves 6–8.

crushed pineapple delight

A marvelous dessert of creamy crushed pineapple with a cookie-crumb crust.

½ cup margarine, softened

1½ cups powdered sugar, plus 2
   tablespoons

2 eggs

1 cup crushed pineapple

1 8-ounce container whipped topping

12 ounces cookies, crushed into
   crumbs

Cream margarine and 1½ cups powdered sugar. Beat in eggs. Add crushed pineapple. In a separate bowl, beat whipped topping with 2 tablespoons powdered sugar and fold into the pineapple mixture. Line a 9x12-inch baking pan with ⅔ of the cookie crumbs. Spread pineapple mixture on top. Sprinkle remaining crumbs on top. Refrigerate.

Serves 12.

banana cookie ice cream

A light, no-fat ice cream that is absolutely delicious.

3 egg whites
3 ripe bananas, sliced (approx. 1
    cup)
⅔ cups sugar
1 teaspoon vanilla extract

1 teaspoon lemon juice
3–4 chocolate cookies, crumbled
⅔ cup coarsely chopped nuts
½ cup chocolate chips, optional

Combine egg whites, bananas, sugar, vanilla, and lemon juice in a mixing bowl. Mix on high speed for 8–10 minutes until volume increases. Fold in crumbled cookies, chopped nuts, and chocolate chips, if desired. Freeze in a covered container.

VARIATIONS

For a richer, ice cream, fold in 1 container of dessert topping, whipped.

Fold in quartered maraschino cherries.

shevi's crème schnitz

*Crème schnitz is an old German recipe which can be made as
individual servings or in a large pan and then cut into squares.*

1 2-pound package puff pastry
   dough
¾ cup cornstarch
4 cups water
3 egg yolks, beaten with a fork
pinch of salt

1 cup sugar
¼ cup margarine
1 tablespoon vanilla
chocolate shavings, sprinkles, maraschino cherries, for garnish

In a bowl, mix together cornstarch and 1 cup water until smooth. Make
sure there are no lumps. Stir in beaten egg yolks and salt. Set aside.
Combine 3 cups water, sugar, and salt in a saucepan. Bring to a boil.
Lower heat and while simmering slowly pour in cornstarch mixture,
stirring constantly until thickened. Remove from fire and stir in margarine and vanilla while mixture is still hot.

Spread puff pastry dough out on a flat surface. Do not roll out. Cut
into rounds with a glass. (For easier cutting, you can dip round edge of
glass into flour.) Place each round on a greased baking pan. Place pan of
rounds into preheated 450° oven and bake for 6–7 minutes until risen.
Lower heat to 350° and continue baking for additional 20 minutes until
golden. Let cool, and with a sharp knife cut each baked round in half.

To assemble schnitz: pour 2 tablespoons of cooled filling on bottom
half. Place top half over it and pour 1 tablespoon of filling over the top.
Decorate tops with shaved chocolate, sprinkles, or cherries. If desired,
all the filling can be put in the middle and the top can be decorated with
melted chocolate or powdered sugar.

Yields 20 schnitz.

VARIATION

In place of above filling, prepare 1 package instant vanilla pudding according to package directions. Fold in 2 8-ounce cartons of whipped
topping and use to fill the schnitz.

deep fried pineapple fritters

A delicious finger food that you — and your kids — will love.

2 eggs, beaten
1 tablespoon sugar
¼ teaspoon salt
¼ teaspoon cinnamon
1 24-ounce can pineapple slices,

with liquid from can
1 teaspoon baking powder
1½ cups flour
oil, for frying

Combine eggs, sugar, salt, cinnamon, liquid from can of pineapple, baking powder, and flour. Mix together until smooth. Dip pineapple slices, whole or halved, into batter and fry in oil on both sides until golden.

Yields 8–10 fritters.

orange-pineapple ices

A light dessert, easy to prepare, without whipped cream or raw eggs.

2 cups water
1 cup sugar
1 package apricot or strawberry
    jello

2 cups orange juice
2 cups pineapple juice

Boil water and sugar together for ½ minute. Stir in jello until thoroughly dissolved. Add fruit juice. Freeze for several hours or overnight. Remove from freezer. Let stand 5 minutes and then mix in mixer for 1–2 minutes. Pour into a square or oblong pan and refreeze. Cut into squares. This can be served with fruit salad or simply cut up fruit on top.

Serves 10–12.

frozen lemon dessert

After a heavy fleishig meal, this fluffy summer dessert will be a real crowd-pleaser.

CRUST

2½ cups graham cracker or cookie crumbs

5 tablespoons margarine, softened to room temperature

¼ cup sugar

FILLING

1 8-ounce carton pareve whipped topping

4 eggs, separated

⅔ cup sugar

⅓ cup lemon juice

1 teaspoon lemon extract

Combine crust ingredients. Press ¾ of mixture into a greased 9-inch baking pan. Reserve some crumbs for sprinkling on top.

To prepare filling, beat whipped topping and set aside. In another bowl, beat egg whites, gradually adding sugar. In a third bowl, beat egg yolks until thick and light. Stir in lemon juice and extract. Fold egg whites into yolks. Then fold in beaten whipped topping. Pour onto crust and sprinkle with reserved crumbs. Freeze.

Serves 8.

TIP

To make a kid-friendly dessert, pour different flavors of jello into muffin tins and allow each child to choose his favorite flavor.

chocolate mousse dessert

A beautiful and luscious dessert that is perfect for Shabbos lunch.
Serve each guest an individual wedge topped with whipped dessert
topping.

6 ounces semi-sweet chocolate
¾ cup margarine
⅓ cup sweet red wine
6 eggs, separated
½ cup powdered sugar

4 tablespoons bread crumbs
jam, for spreading on top
1 8-ounce container dessert
    topping

Melt chocolate and margarine and add wine. Beat egg yolks until light. Stir in melted chocolate-margarine mixture. In another bowl, beat whites until frothy. Add ¼ cup powdered sugar and beat until stiff. Fold whites into chocolate mixture. Divide mixture into two parts. Fold bread crumbs into one part and pour into a 8–9-inch round baking pan. Bake in a 350° oven for 20–25 minutes. Remove from oven and spread jam on top. Spread second half of chocolate mixture on top of jam. Beat dessert topping, adding ¼ cup powdered sugar, and spread over baked chocolate mixture. Refrigerate. Serve chilled.

Serves 8–10.

CAKES
& ICINGS

old-fashioned chocolate cake

A quick, easy, and tasty recipe for classic chocolate cake.

¾ cup margarine
1½ cups sugar
4 eggs
½ cup cocoa
½ cup sweet red wine

¾ cup water
2 teaspoons vanilla extract
2½ cups flour
2 teaspoons baking powder
½ teaspoon baking soda

Cream margarine and sugar. Beat in eggs until creamy. Add cocoa, wine, water, and vanilla. Blend in flour, baking powder, and baking soda. Pour mixture into a lined 9x13-inch pan. Bake in a preheated 350° oven for 35–40 minutes. Frost with chocolate icing, if desired.

Serves 12–14.

CHOCOLATE ICING

2 cups powdered sugar
3 tablespoons cocoa
1 teaspoon vanilla

2 tablespoons margarine
3 tablespoons water

Mix all ingredients together until creamy.

special marble cake

This versatile, classic marble cake is a sure hit, with or without chocolate frosting. The powdered sugar lends it a light touch of sweetness.

3 cups flour
¼ teaspoon salt
3 teaspoons baking powder
4 eggs, separated
1 cup powdered sugar
1 cup granulated sugar
1 cup orange juice
1 cup oil
1 tablespoon vanilla extract

CHOCOLATE SYRUP

⅓ cup cocoa
½ cup sugar
½ cup hot water
1 teaspoon vanilla extract

QUICK AND EASY FROSTING

3 ounces chocolate
2 tablespoons water
1–2 tablespoons margarine or oil

Combine flour, salt, and baking powder and set aside. Beat egg whites until frothy. Gradually add powdered sugar and granulated sugar and beat until stiff. In another bowl, beat egg yolks until light and fluffy. Add orange juice, oil, and vanilla extract. Blend flour mixture into yolks. Fold in stiffly beaten egg whites. In a small bowl, combine all the ingredients for chocolate syrup and beat until smooth. Blend syrup mixture into ⅓ of the batter. Pour ½ of the remaining white batter into a greased 10-inch tube pan. Pour chocolate batter on top. Pour remaining white mixture over chocolate mixture. To marbleize cut through batter at 2-inch intervals. Bake in a preheated 350° oven for 1 hour. Or assemble in a 9x13-inch pan and bake for 45–50 minutes.

For a quick and tasty frosting, melt chocolate and combine with water and margarine or oil. Pour over cooled cake and spread with a hot knife. To prevent it from losing its sheen, let it cool at room temperature, not in the refrigerator.

Serves 12–14.

roulada with cream filling

A jelly roll with a chocolate cream filling.

CAKE
5 eggs, separated
1 cup sugar
3 tablespoons oil
5 levels tablespoons flour
1 teaspoon baking powder

1½ tablespoons cocoa

FILLING
1 8-ounce container whipped topping
5 ounces chocolate (milk or dark), melted

Whip egg whites until frothy. Gradually add sugar and continue beating until stiff. Stir in oil. Fold in egg yolks, flour, baking powder, and cocoa. Spread on cookie sheet or 11x17-inch baking pan lined with baking paper. Bake in a preheated 325° oven for 20 minutes until slightly golden. Remove carefully from baking pan and place on a clean dish towel. Roll up immediately, together with the towel, from the long end. Meanwhile, beat the whipped topping and fold in melted chocolate. Unroll the cake and spread with filling, reserving about 4 tablespoons for top. Roll cake up again. Spread reserved chocolate filling over top of roll. Refrigerate until ready to serve. Cut into slices to serve.

Serves 12–14.

VARIATION

Fill dough with ice cream instead of chocolate cream and freeze.

TIP

To make chocolate curls, hold a bar of chocolate in the palm of your hand and scrape chocolate off into curls with a vegetable peeler.

deluxe sponge cake

*My neighbor used to bring me this delightful sponge cake every year
on Purim. A light and airy cake with only 1 tablespoon oil and a
third less flour and sugar than chiffon cake, it can be enjoyed even
by dieters. Try it and see!*

7 large eggs, room temperature,
   separated

1 cup sugar

1 tablespoon oil

2 teaspoons vanilla extract

juice and grated rind of 1 lemon or
   orange

¼ teaspoon salt

1 teaspoon baking powder

1 cup flour

In a mixing bowl beat egg yolks, gradually adding sugar, until light,
about 5 minutes. Stir in oil, vanilla extract, lemon or orange juice, and
rind, and salt and beat another 1–2 minutes. Blend in baking powder
and flour until just combined. In a separate bowl, beat egg whites until
stiff and fold into the first mixture. Pour into a greased 10-inch tube
pan. Bake in a preheated 325° oven for 1 hour. Remove from oven and
invert on a bottle. Let stand until cool.

Serves 12–14.

VARIATION

Plum-Topped Sponge Cake: Slice 4–5 fresh plums and place, cut
side up, on top of batter in pan. Bake as directed. The juice of the
plums will run down the cake. Delicious and different.

Filled Sponge Cake: Place whole sponge cake on a round platter,
upside down. Slice off top of cake about 1 inch from the top. Remove
and set aside. With a sharp knife, cut out inside of cake, leaving a wall
about 1 inch thick. Fill cavity with whipped cream combined with ½
cup of toasted slivered almonds. Replace top of cake. Frost top and
sides of cake with remaining whipped cream. Sprinkle top and sides
with toasted slivered almonds or chocolate chips.

ⓟ

hungarian coffee cake

A Hungarian housewife's delight, this cake consists of small round balls
of yeast dough dipped in a sugar-cinnamon mix and placed together to
form a round cake with a bumpy texture. A taste of Gan Eden!

½ recipe Special Yeast Dough (see
　　Pastries, Pies, and Cheesecakes)
½ cup olive oil, melted butter, or
　　melted margarine

2 teaspoons cinnamon
¾ cup sugar
1 cup chopped nuts

Instead of filling your dough and rolling as for jelly roll, roll it out and
pinch off pieces 1½ inches in length. Roll dough with the palms of
your hands into balls and dip into melted butter, or margarine, then
into cinnamon, sugar, and chopped nuts. Place balls in a greased 9-inch
round baking pan, touching each other in two layers. Let rise about 45
minutes. Bake in a preheated 375° oven for 35–40 minutes.

Serves 12–14.

ⓟ

nut cake with grated chocolate

Chocolate, nuts, and juice come together in this unique, filling cake.

6 eggs, separated
1½ cups sugar
½ cup oil
2 teaspoons vanilla extract
¼ teaspoon salt

½ cup grape juice
1½ cups flour
1½ teaspoons baking powder
1 cup chopped walnuts
2 ounces grated chocolate

Beat egg yolks with 1 cup sugar until light. Add oil, vanilla, salt, and
grape juice and mix on low speed. Stir in flour, baking powder, walnuts,
and chocolate. Beat until combined, but make sure not to overmix. In
another bowl, beat egg whites, gradually adding remaining ½ cup sugar,
beating until stiff. Gently fold into batter. Pour into a lined 9x13-inch
baking pan. Bake in a preheated 350° oven for 45 minutes.

Serves 10–12.

cinnamon cake

For cinnamon lovers and for everyone else, too: a marvelous crumb cake with a spectacular flavor.

3 eggs

1½ cups sugar

¾ cup oil

1 teaspoon vanilla extract

¾ cup orange juice

2½ cups flour

3 teaspoons baking power

¼ teaspoon salt

CRUMB TOPPING

½ cup brown sugar

2 teaspoons cinnamon

1 tablespoon margarine

2 teaspoons flour

⅓ cup walnuts, chopped

Beat eggs until light, then add sugar and beat again. Stir in oil, vanilla, and orange juice. Blend in flour, baking powder, and salt. Pour half of mixture into a greased Bundt pan or 10-inch tube pan. In a separate bowl, combine the ingredients for the topping. Sprinkle half the topping over the cake in the pan. Pour remaining half of batter into pan and sprinkle remaining half of topping on top. Bake in a preheated 350° oven for about 50 minutes until golden brown on top.

Serves 14.

honey orange date cake

This healthier cake is a nice choice for Rosh HaShanah,
when honey is used so freely.

3 eggs
½ cup brown sugar
½ cup white sugar
¾ cup honey
½ cup oil
½ teaspoon salt
¾ cup strong coffee
grated rind of ½ a lemon
grated rind of ½ an orange

2 tablespoons brandy
½ cup raisins
1 cup dates, diced
1 teaspoon cinnamon
½ teaspoon ginger or nutmeg
2 teaspoons baking powder
¾ teaspoon baking soda
3 cups flour, sifted

In an electric mixer bowl, beat eggs until frothy. Slowly beat in brown and white sugar. Stir in honey, oil, salt, coffee, grated lemon and orange rind, brandy, raisins, dates, cinnamon, and ginger or nutmeg. Blend in baking powder, baking soda, and sifted flour. Pour into a greased 9x13-inch baking pan. Bake in a preheated 350° oven for 45 minutes. When cool, cut into squares.

Yields 24–30 squares.

TIP

It is a good idea to soak raisins for cakes in
warm water before using them, to make them
plump and juicy. (With Israeli raisins, you'll do
this anyway as a preliminary step
to checking them.)

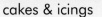

date-nut cake

A delicious, wholesome recipe.

¾ cup margarine
1¼ cups sugar
4 eggs, separated
¾ cup orange juice
2 teaspoons vanilla extract
2 cups flour

1 teaspoon baking powder
1 teaspoon baking soda
1 apple, shredded
1½ cups chopped dates
¾ cup coarsely chopped walnuts

Cream margarine and sugar well. Beat in eggs yolks, orange juice, and vanilla. Blend in flour, baking powder, and baking soda. Add shredded apple, chopped dates, and walnuts. In a separate bowl, beat egg whites until stiff and fold into mixture. Pour mixture into a greased Bundt pan or 9- or 10-inch tube pan, and bake in a preheated 350° oven for 1 hour.

Serves 12.

(Can also be made without separating the eggs. Just beat in whole eggs.)

prize apple cake

A thick layer of sliced apples in this delicious cake makes it almost like an apple pie.

1 cup margarine	2 teaspoons vanilla extract
3 cups flour	1½ teaspoons baking powder
2 cups sugar	2 pounds apples, peeled and sliced
2 eggs, beaten	2 teaspoons cinnamon

Cut margarine into flour with pastry cutter or two knives until it resembles peas. Add 1½ cups sugar, eggs, vanilla, and baking powder. Divide dough in half. Roll out one half and spread onto a greased 9x13-inch baking pan. Scatter the sliced apples on top. Mix togther ½ cup sugar and cinammon and sprinkle over apples. Roll out remaining dough and place on top of apples. Bake in a preheated 350° oven for 45 minutes.

apple streusel

A quick, easy, and delicious recipe.

2 eggs	6 apples, peeled and sliced
¾ cup sugar	**TOPPING**
½ cup oil	½ cup margarine
½ cup orange juice	½ cup sugar
2½ cups flour	¼ teaspoon salt
2½ teaspoons baking powder	1 cup flour

Beat eggs. Add sugar, oil, orange juice, flour, and baking powder. Spread the dough into a greased 9x13-inch baking pan. Arrange sliced apples on top. Mix together the ingredients for the streusel topping and sprinkle on top. Bake in a preheated 350° oven for 45 minutes.

Yields 16–20 squares.

peach-topped cake

A multi-tiered dessert cake with a jello topping enveloping sliced peaches. Your company is sure to love this one.

1 cup margarine
1½ cups sugar
5 eggs, separated
1 cup orange juice
1 teaspoon vanilla extract
2 cups flour
2 teaspoons baking powder
½ cup water

1 28-ounce can sliced peaches, with liquid
1 8-ounce container whipped topping
½ package instant vanilla pudding mix
1 package pineapple jello
2 cups boiling water

Beat margarine with ¾ cup sugar. Add egg yolks, orange juice, and vanilla. Blend in flour and baking powder. In another bowl, beat egg whites, gradually adding remaining ¾ cup sugar until stiff. Fold egg white mixture into egg yolk mixture. Pour into a greased 11x17-inch baking pan or cookie sheet. Bake in a preheated 350° for 40–45 minutes.

Combine ¼ cup of liquid from peaches and ½ cup water and pour over baked cake while still warm to make it moist. Whip topping and add instant pudding. Spread mixture on top of cake. Place peach slices on top in rows. Prepare jello by mixing it with boiling water. Let cool and pour over top of peaches. Refrigerate immediately until set. Cut into squares or rectangles.

VARIATION

Strawberry-Topped Cake: Use 2½ cups of halved fresh strawberries instead of peaches, and any juice instead of liquid from peaches.

zucchini cake

A glorious cake chock-full of raisins and nuts, with maraschino cherries and dates to add extra flavor.

¾ cup oil

1½ cups sugar

3 eggs

2 teaspoons vanilla extract

2 cups flour, sifted

½ teaspoon salt

1 teaspoon baking soda

1 teaspoon baking powder

1 cup chopped walnuts

1 teaspoon cinnamon

½ teaspoon nutmeg

1 cup white raisins

1 cup chopped dates

2 cups shredded zucchini

¾ cup maraschino cherries, halved

TOPPING

½ cup brown sugar

3 tablespoons oil or margarine

2 tablespoons water

1 teaspoon vanilla extract

In a large bowl, combine oil, sugar, eggs, and vanilla and beat well. Stir in flour, salt, baking soda, and baking powder. Add remaining ingredients. Do not overmix. Pour into a greased and floured tube pan. Bake in a preheated 350° oven for 1 hour until golden brown.

While cake is baking, combine brown sugar, oil or margarine, and water for topping in a saucepan. Cook for 2 minutes. Remove from heat and add vanilla. When cake is ready, remove from oven and turn upside down onto a platter, removing baking pan. While still warm, drizzle topping over cake.

Serves 12.

TIP

If a cake rises in the center and not around the edge, or if top is cracked: 1) Insufficient liquid was used; 2) the batter was mixed too much after adding the flour; or 3) the oven was too hot at the beginning of the baking.

food processor banana cake

Moist and tasty, this cake can be made in the food processor for less hassle and is an excellent way of using up overripe fruit. For variation, use cut-up pears, peaches, or apricots.

3 eggs
1 cup brown sugar
½ cup white sugar
¾ cup oil
¼ teaspoon salt
2 teaspoons vanilla extract

3 large bananas, cut up (about 1 cup)
1 cup whole wheat flour
1½ cups white flour
2½ teaspoons baking powder
½ cup raisins, optional

Pour eggs, brown sugar, white sugar, oil, salt, and vanilla into food processor and process until smooth. Add bananas and process with on-off bursts until bananas are small. Combine flour, baking powder, and baking soda in a separate bowl. Pour in banana mixture and mix together until well blended. Add raisins, if desired. Pour into a well-greased 9x13-inch baking pan and bake in a preheated 350° oven for 40–45 minutes.

Serves 12–14.

VARIATION

Substitute 1–1½ cups fresh peaches, apricots, pears, or other fruits for the bananas.

halvah cake

This cake is one of my personal favorites — and anyone who enjoys halvah will echo my sentiments.

BOTTOM LAYER
1 cup margarine, scant
½ cup sugar
4 egg yolks
generous pinch of salt
2½ cups flour
2½ teaspoons baking powder

FILLING
7 ounces halvah

4 tablespoons sugar
4 tablespoons cocoa
4 tablespoons water
½ cup margarine
3 tablespoons cognac

TOPPING
4 egg whites
½ cup sugar
3½ ounces shredded coconut

Cream margarine with sugar. Stir in egg yolks. Add salt, flour, and baking powder. Spread evenly into a lined 9x13-inch baking pan.

In a saucepan cook all filling ingredients except margarine and cognac until halvah is dissolved. Remove from heat and stir in margarine and cognac. Spread over bottom layer.

In a mixing bowl, beat egg whites for topping until frothy. Gradually add sugar and continue beating until mixture can stand up in stiff peaks. Gently fold in coconut. Spread topping on top of filling and bake in a preheated 350° oven for 45 minutes. When cool, cut into squares with a sharp, warm knife.

Serves 20.

sugar-free oatmeal muffins

For those with sugar restrictions — give these delicious and filling muffins a try. Your whole family will love them.

3 eggs, beaten
1 cup Splenda
½ cup oil
1 teaspoon vanilla extract
1 tablespoon honey
2 cups plain yogurt
2 cups fine oatmeal
1 cup whole wheat flour

1 cup white flour
2 teaspoons baking powder
¼ cup sesame seeds
¼ cup sunflower seeds
½ cup raisins
½ cup coarsely chopped nuts, optional

In a mixing bowl combine eggs, Splenda, oil, vanilla, honey, yogurt, and oatmeal. Blend in whole wheat and white flour and baking powder. Stir in the sunflower seeds, raisins, and nuts. Pour into greased muffin tins and bake in a preheated 350° oven for about 20 minutes.

Yields 30–35 muffins.

strawberry sauce

To be used over ice cream or top of cake.

½ cup sugar
1 cup mashed strawberries
¾ cup water

2 tablespoons cornstarch
¼ cup water

Combine sugar, strawberry purée, and water in a saucepan. Bring to a boil. Dissolve cornstarch in ¼ cup water and stir into simmering mixture only until slightly thickened. Remove from heat and let cool. Pour cooled sauce over cake.

extra-special icings

*Here are some extra-special icings
to add that extra-special touch to your cake.*

CARAMEL ICING

2 cups brown sugar
⅔ cup water
pinch of salt

1 teaspoon vanilla extract
2 tablespoons margarine

Combine brown sugar and water in a saucepan. Cook for several minutes to soft ball stage (remove about half a teaspoon and with fingers form into soft ball). Remove from heat and let cool slightly. Stir in margarine and vanilla and beat until thickened. Spread on cake immediately.

ORANGE ICING

2 cups powdered sugar
pinch of salt
grated rind of 1 orange

3 tablespoons orange juice
2-3 tablespoons margarine

Combine all ingredients and spread on cooled cake.

PEANUT BUTTER ICING

2 cups powdered sugar
2 tablespoons oil
pinch of salt

3 tablespoons orange juice
½ cup creamy peanut butter

Mix all ingredients together and beat well. If necessary, add a little more powdered sugar until spreading consistency. Spread on cooled cake.

COOKIES
& BARS

MORE THAN
A TASTE OF HONEY

Since the Middle Ages, young Jewish children have been introduced to the study of the Torah by writing the letters of the alef beis on a slate and covering them with honey. The child then licked the honeyed letters with his tongue, discovering that the words of Torah are as sweet as honey.

Honey is excellent for baking because it retains moisture, keeping baked goods from drying out. It helps to keep them fresher longer. It also gives a chewier texture and a rich brown color to cakes and cookies.

Clover honey, one of the most popular kinds of honey for baking and table use, is light in color and mild in flavor. Buckwheat honey is dark and more strongly flavored. Both are of equal quality, however, and are easily digestible.

Honey is sweeter and more caloric than sugar. One tablespoon of sugar has 50 calories, whereas the same amount of honey has 64 calories. Even so, honey is more nutritious than the granulated stuff and far more easily digested. Honey contains more potassium, iron, and sodium than sugar does.

The Rambam points out that a tablespoon of honey in a glass of warm water before breakfast is an excellent aid to the digestive process. Tosafos, a commentary of the Talmud, refers to honey as a preservative of fruits.

regal peanut butter balls

*A luscious, no-bake confection, these are the perfect choice
for a Kiddush or mishloach manos.*

1 cup sugar	4 cups quick oats
½ cup pareve cream	1 tablespoon vanilla extract
½ cup margarine	½ cup raisins
4 tablespoons cocoa	shreded coconut
½ cup chunky peanut butter	finely chopped nuts, for coating balls

In a saucepan, heat sugar, pareve cream, margarine, and cocoa until
blended. Remove from heat and stir in peanut butter, oats, vanilla, and
raisins. With floured hands, roll into balls. Roll half the balls in coconut
and half in chopped nuts. Store in a square or rectangular container.

peanut bars dipped in melted chocolate

*Dip these two layers of sweetness and crunch in melted chocolate
after baking for a finishing touch.*

½ cup margarine	jam, for spreading on top
¾ cup sugar	melted chocolate, for dipping
2 eggs	**PEANUT TOPPING**
2 teaspoons vanilla extract	¾ cup margarine
2½ cups flour	¾ cup sugar
3 teaspoons baking powder	4 tablespoons water
¼ teaspoon salt	1 cup coarsely chopped peanuts

Cream margarine and sugar. Beat in eggs and vanilla. Add flour, baking
powder, and salt. Spread dough on a lined 11x17-inch cookie sheet.
Spread with jam. For peanut topping, combine margarine, sugar, and
water in a saucepan and bring to a boil. Remove from heat and stir in
chopped peanuts. Spread on top of jam in pan. Bake in a preheated
350° oven. Cut into rectangles and dip each side in melted chocolate.
Place on a rack or plate to dry.

chocolate peanut butter bars

*In these mouth-watering bars, the peanut butter filling is
sandwiched between layes of marbleized chocolate dough to create a
luscious bar with a sensational taste.*

DOUGH
1 cup margarine
2 cups sugar
4 eggs
1 tablespoon vanilla extract
1½ cups flour
¾ cup cocoa
1 teaspoon baking powder

¼ teaspoon salt
1 cup chocolate chips

PEANUT BUTTER FILLING
⅓ cup margarine
⅓ cup sugar
2 eggs
¾ cup peanut butter
1 teaspoon vanilla extract

Cream margarine and sugar. Beat in eggs and vanilla. Stir in flour, cocoa, baking powder, and salt. If necessary, add a little more flour to
make dough. Divide dough in half. Spread ½ of dough into a greased
9x13-inch baking pan. Cream margarine and sugar for filling, then beat
in remaining ingredients. Spread over dough in pan. Roll out second
half of dough and place on top of filling. Sprinkle with chocolate chips.
Place in preheated 350° oven for 5 minutes to melt chocolate chips.
Remove from oven and marbelize chocolate chips with a knife. Bake at
350° for about 30 minutes.

Yields 24–30 bars.

T I P

*For better results in baking, preheat your oven
for ten minutes before putting in the pan of
cake or cookies.*

fabulous peanut butter delights

We make these bars every time we have a family simchah.
They are an absolute favorite.

⅔ cup margarine
⅔ cup brown sugar
1 egg
1 teaspoon vanilla extract
½ cup flour
½ teaspoon baking powder
½ teaspoon baking soda
½ teaspoon salt

TOPPING
½ cup powdered sugar
1½ cups crunchy peanut butter
¼ cup margarine
1 teaspoon vanilla extract
8 ounces chocolate chips, melted,
    for spreading on top

Cream margarine and brown sugar. Beat in egg and vanilla. Stir in flour, baking powder, baking soda, and salt. Spread mixture into a greased baking pan and bake in a preheated 350° oven for 15 minutes. Mix together topping ingredients except chocolate chips until well mixed and spread on top of baked crust. Freeze until firm. Melt chocolate chips and spread evenly on top. Cut into squares.

Yields 24 squares.

T I P

For lower calories, substitute equal amounts of
Splenda to replace sugar.

halvah-nut triangles

I enjoy serving these delightful triangles for dessert at my Purim seudah. You can also send them in your mishloach manos — expect rave reviews!

1½ cups margarine

1½ cups sugar, plus 3 tablespoons

3 egg yolks

⅔ cup chopped nuts

½ cup sweet red wine

4 cups flour

3 teaspoons baking powder

3 tablespoons cocoa

½ cup jam

HALVAH LAYER

3½ ounces plain halvah

3 tablespoons sugar

2 teaspoons vanilla extract

¼ cup water

3 tablespoons cocoa

¼ cup margarine

3 tablespoons cocoa

3 tablespoons sugar

¼ cup pecan halves for garnish

Cream margarine, 1½ cups sugar, and egg yolks until fluffy. Add chopped nuts, wine, flour, and baking powder. Divide dough in half. Stir cocoa and remaining sugar into one half and spread it on a greased 9x13-inch baking pan. Spread jam on top. Spread remaining half of dough evenly on top of jam. Bake in a 350° oven for 30 minutes.

Meanwhile, prepare halvah layer as follows: In a saucepan, cook together halvah, sugar, vanilla, water, and cocoa for 2 minutes. Remove from heat and stir in margarine. While still warm, spread halvah mixture on top of bars. Combine cocoa and sugar for topping and sprinkle on top of halvah. Cut into triangles. If desired, place half a pecan on top of each triangle.

Yields 24 triangles.

multi-mix bars

A marvelous, margarine-free recipe made with coconut, raisins, and nuts. Sprinkled with chocolate chips after baking for a beautiful, appetizing confection.

1 cup oil
2½ cups brown sugar
3 eggs
3 cups flour
1½ teaspoons baking powder
¾ teaspoon baking soda

2 teaspoons vanilla extract
⅔ cup coarsely chopped nuts
⅔ cup shredded coconut
½ cup raisins
1 cup chocolate chips

Beat together oil, brown sugar, and eggs. Stir in flour, baking powder, baking soda, and vanilla. Add chopped nuts, shredded coconut, and raisins. Pour into a lined 9x13-inch baking pan. Sprinkle with chocolate chips. Bake in a preheated 350° oven for 30 minutes.

Yields 24–30 bars.

T I P

To prevent fruit or raisins from sinking to the bottom of a cake, shake the fruit in a little flour before adding it to the cake batter.

yummy bars

Made with a topping of chocolate chips, jam, and nuts, these scrumptious squares can be made thicker or thinner, depending on the size of the pan you use for baking.

3 cups flour

¾ cup margarine

1½ cups sugar

½ cup brown sugar

2 teaspoons baking powder

1 cup quick oats

TOPPING

3–4 tablespoons jam

2 cups chocolate chips

½ cup coarsely chopped walnuts

Place flour in a bowl. Cut margarine into flour until it becomes the size of peas. Stir in white sugar, brown sugar, baking powder, and oats. Reserve ½ cup of mixture. Pat remainder of mixture onto an 11x17-inch cookie sheet. Bake in a preheated 350° oven for 10 minutes. Spread jam on top. Sprinkle chocolate chips on top of jam. Combine chopped walnuts with ½ cup of reserved mixture and sprinkle on top. Bake an additional 15 minutes. Let cool and cut into small squares or rectangles. Place into fluted paper cups.

These make very thin squares. For a thicker version bake in a 9x13-inch baking pan.

Yields 48–60 bars.

brownies

A rich chocolatey favorite.

4 eggs
2 cups sugar
1 cup canola oil
¼ teaspoon salt
2 teaspoons vanilla extract

1 cup cocoa or 4 ounces baking
    chocolate, melted
1¼ cups flour
1 teaspoon baking powder, optional
¾ cup coarsely chopped walnuts

Beat eggs until foamy, gradually adding sugar, oil, salt, and vanilla. Stir in cocoa or baking chocolate and blend in flour and baking powder, being careful not to overbeat. Gently stir in chopped walnuts. (Alternatively, chopped nuts can be sprinkled on top before baking, instead of being folded into batter.) Pour into a lined 9x13-inch baking pan. Bake in a preheated 350° oven for 25 minutes. Let cool before cutting.

Yields 30 brownies.

VARIATION

Rum Brownies: Use 1 teaspoon rum flavoring in place of vanilla.

Note: Eliminating the baking powder will make a moister brownie.

whole wheat brownies

A slightly healthier version of the brownie recipe above, these excellent brownies call for whole wheat flour and brown sugar. Enjoy your brownies without the guilt!

4 eggs
2 cups brown sugar
¾ cup olive oil
2 teaspoons vanilla extract

1 cup cocoa, scant
1¼ cups whole wheat flour
½ teaspoon baking powder

Follow brownie instructions above.

Yields 30 brownies.

hungarian filbert bars with fluffy chocolate topping

An old Hungarian recipe that is very special. This confection was served at a sheva berachos I attended, made by a neighbor of the hostess. After indulging in this chocolate dream, I knew it was a recipe that I had to have. The neighbor graciously shared it with me, and now I pass it on to my readers.

BOTTOM LAYER
¾ cup margarine
¾ cup sugar
1 egg
1 egg yolk
1 cup ground filberts
1½ cups flour
1½ teaspoons baking powder
¼ teaspoon salt

⅓ cup jam, for spreading on dough

TOP LAYER
6 ounces semi-sweet chocolate
2 tablespoons water
5 eggs, separated
pinch of salt
1 teaspoon vanilla extract
½ cup sugar

Combine ingredients for bottom layer and pat into a greased 10x15-inch baking pan. Bake in a preheated 350° oven for 15 minutes. Spread with jam and bake 5 more minutes.

Meanwhile, melt chocolate for the top layer in a saucepan. Add water and stir. Remove from heat. Beat egg yolks and stir into cooled chocolate mixture. Add salt and vanilla. In a separate bowl, beat egg whites until stiff, gradually adding the sugar, and fold into chocolate mixture. Spread mixture on prebaked crust and bake at 350° for 30 minutes more.

Yields 24 bars.

viennese squares

A family simchah special, these scrumptious squares are consistently well-received. A real crowd-pleaser!

FIRST LAYER
½ cup margarine
½ cup brown sugar
2 cups flour

1 cup coarsely chopped nuts
1 cup shredded coconut
2 teaspoons vanilla extract
¼ teaspoon salt

SECOND LAYER
6 eggs
3 cups brown sugar
4 tablespoons flour

LEMON ICING
2 cups powdered sugar
2 tablespoons margarine
4 tablespoons lemon juice

Mix together margarine, brown sugar, and flour for first layer. Mixture will be crumbly. Spread in a greased 9x13-inch baking pan. Bake in a preheated 350° oven for 25 minutes. Meanwhile, beat eggs for the second layer until light, adding brown sugar. Stir in flour, chopped nuts, coconut, vanilla, and salt. Spread on the first layer while it is still warm. Bake an additional 25–30 minutes. Let cool. Mix together ingredients for lemon icing and spread on top.

Yields 24–30 squares.

T I P

To keep brown sugar from drying out, store it in a tightly covered jar with a slice of fresh white bread.

chocolate oat bars

Incredibly easy to prepare, this recipe combines the crunch of the sugared oats with a delicious peanut butter and chocolate topping to make an all-around terrific bar.

⅔ cup margarine

1 cup brown sugar

½ cup corn syrup or honey

1 tablespoon vanilla extract

4 cups uncooked quick oats

TOPPING

6 ounces chocolate chips

⅔ cup crunchy peanut butter

Cream margarine and sugar. Stir in corn syrup or honey, vanilla, and oats. Spread in a well-greased 9x13-inch baking pan. Bake in a preheated 350° oven for 15 minutes. Let cool. For topping, melt chocolate chips with peanut butter over low heat. Spread over baked oatmeal crust. Cut into bars or rectangles.

Yields 24–30 bars.

chocolate nut squares

So simple — and so scrumptious.

1 cup margarine

1½ cups brown sugar

1 egg

1 teaspoon vanilla extract

2 cups flour

6 ounces baking chocolate, melted

¾ cup chopped walnuts

Cream margarine and brown sugar. Beat in egg and vanilla. Add flour. Pat mixture into a greased 9-inch square baking pan. Bake in a preheated 350° oven for about 10–12 minutes. Remove from oven and spread melted chocolate evenly on top. Sprinkle with chopped walnuts. Let cool and cut into squares.

Yields 24 squares.

poppy seed nut squares

A very special recipe with a fantastic flavor, this cake can be cut into small squares and put into fancy cupcake holders for a Kiddush or reception.

DOUGH

1½ cups margarine

½ cup sugar

6 egg yolks

1⅓ ounces dry yeast, diluted in ¼ cup lukewarm water

juice of ½ a lemon

6 cups flour

1 whole egg, beaten, for spreading on top

POPPY SEED FILLING

10 ounces poppy seeds, ground

1½ cups sugar

4 tablespoons honey

½ cup water

4 tablespoons margarine

grated rind of 2 lemons

NUT FILLING

1 pound (2 cups) nuts, finely chopped

1½ cups sugar

juice of 2 lemons

To make dough, cream margarine and sugar. Beat in egg yolks, yeast mixture, and lemon juice. Blend in flour. Refrigerate several hours or overnight.

To make poppy seed filling, combine poppy seeds, sugar, honey, and water in a saucepan and cook for about 7 minutes, stirring constantly. Remove from fire and stir in margarine and grated lemon rind.

For nut filling, combine chopped nuts with sugar and lemon juice. Mixture should be moist. If not, add a little more lemon juice.

Assemble cake by rolling out ⅓ of dough on a large 11x17-inch cookie sheet. Spread poppy seed filling evenly over dough. Roll out second ⅓ of dough and place it on top. Spread a layer of nut filling over this dough. Roll out third piece of dough and place on top of nut filling. Smear top layer of dough with a beaten whole egg. Bake in a preheated 350° oven for 45–50 minutes. Let cool and cut into small squares.

Yields 24–30 squares.

apple and jam crisps

*A sweet, delicious treat guaranteed to be enjoyed
by children and adults alike.*

¾ cup margarine
¾ cup brown sugar
1½ teaspoons baking soda
1 teaspoon vanilla extract
⅓ teaspoon salt
2 eggs
1½ cups flour

FILLING
1 cup raspberry jam
1 cup walnuts, coarsely chopped
¾ cup raisins
5 apples, peeled and sliced

TOPPING
¼ cup sugar
1 teaspoon cinnamon

Combine margarine, sugar, baking soda, vanilla, salt, and eggs. Mix well.
Stir in flour. Divide dough in half. Wrap each half in a plastic bag and
freeze overnight. When ready to bake, grate ½ of dough into a 9x13-inch
baking pan. Mix together jam, nuts, raisins, and apples and spread mixture over dough. Cut or grate second half of dough on top of jam mixture. Combine sugar and cinnamon and sprinkle over dough. Bake in a
preheated 350° oven for 45 minutes. Let cool and cut into squares.

Yields 24 squares.

crispy bars

*My granddaughter Chanie brought this recipe from London. A
delightful thin crisp square made with oatmeal, coconuts, and honey.*

¾ cup margarine
1½ tablespoons honey
1 teaspoon baking soda
1 cup sugar

2 cups quick oats
1 cup flour
1 cup shredded coconut
1 egg, beaten

Melt margarine and honey. Stir in baking soda. Add remaining dry ingredients. Stir in egg. Spread mixture in a 10x17-inch greased cookie
sheet. Bake in preheated 350° oven for 20 minutes.

Yields 40 bars.

cranberry-nut squares

*A uniquely delicious cranberry-nut filling with a sweet
and crunchy oat-bar base.*

1½ cups quick oats
1 cup brown sugar
1½ cups flour
¾ cup margarine
pinch of salt
½ teaspoon baking soda

FILLING
1 can cranberry sauce
½ cup crushed pineapple, drained
½ cup chopped nuts
¼ teaspoon vanilla extract

Mix together oatmeal, sugar, flour, margarine, salt, and baking soda
until well blended. Spread ½ of mixture in a greased 7x11-inch baking
pan. Combine filling ingredients and spread evenly on top of the crust.
Sprinkle remaining oat mixture on top. Bake in a preheated 375° oven
for 25–30 minutes. Let cool and cut into squares.

Yields 24 squares.

eggless apricot bars

An excellent bar for those with egg restrictions.

1½ cups flour
1 teaspoon baking powder
¼ teaspoon salt
¾ cup margarine

1 cup brown sugar, packed
1½ cups quick oats
¾ cup apricot jam

Mix together flour, baking powder, and salt. Cut in margarine with a
table knife. Stir in brown sugar and oats until crumbly. Spread ⅔ of
mixture in a lined 9x12-inch baking pan. Spread jam on top, and cover
with remaining ⅓ of oat mixture. Bake in a preheated 350° oven for
about 35 minutes until golden brown. Let cool and cut into bars.

Yields 24 bars.

(P)

whole-grain health cookies

With whole wheat flour, sunflower seeds, sesame seeds, nuts, minimal sugar, and no margarine, you can enjoy this delicious cookie without qualms. It is also egg-free, making it ideal for those watching their cholesterol intake.

¾ cup oil	3 cups quick oats
1 cup brown sugar	4 tablespoons boiling water
2½ teaspoons vanilla sugar	½ cup coarsely chopped walnuts
1 cup whole wheat flour	¼ cup sesame seeds
1½ teaspoons baking powder	¼ cup sunflower seeds

Mix together oil, sugar, and vanilla sugar. Add remaining ingredients. Drop by rounded teaspoonfuls on a greased baking sheet, two inches apart. Bake in a 350° oven for 15 minutes.

Yields 3 dozen cookies.

(P)

flourless oatmeal cookies

Ideal for those allergic to wheat.

3 eggs	½ teaspoon salt
1 cup sugar	1 cup shredded coconut
2 tablespoons oil	2 cups quick oats
1 teaspoon vanilla extract	

Combine all ingredients. Line a cookie sheet with baking paper and drop dough by half-teaspoonfuls onto the cookie sheet. Bake in a pre-heated 350° oven for 10 minutes.

Yields about 25 cookies.

white chocolate chip cookies

*A pleasant change from the classic chocolate chip cookie, these cookies
are simply delicious — you'll want to make them often.*

1 cup margarine	½ teaspoon salt
1 cup brown sugar	½ cup cocoa
¾ cup white sugar	1 teaspoon baking soda
2 eggs	2¼ cups flour
1 teaspoon vanilla extract	6 ounces white chocolate chips

Cream margarine and sugars. Beat in eggs. Stir in remaining ingredients. Shape into balls the size of a walnut and place on a lined cookie
sheet. Press down slightly with a fork. Bake in a preheated 350° oven
for 10 minutes.

Yields about 36 cookies.

fruit spice cookies

*These delicious cookies can be made with whole wheat flour, making
them even healthier.*

½ cup margarine	2 teaspoons cinnamon
¾ cup brown sugar	¼ teaspoon ground cloves
2 eggs	¼ teaspoon allspice
¼ cup sweet red wine	⅛ teaspoon salt
1 cups whole wheat flour	¾ cup coarsely chopped walnuts
½ cup white flour	¾ cup raisins, chopped dates, or
½ teaspoon baking soda	chopped candied citron

Cream margarine and brown sugar until light. Add eggs and wine and
beat well. Blend in flour, baking soda, cinnamon, cloves, allspice, and
salt. Stir in walnuts and fruit. Drop mixture from a teaspoon onto a
greased or lined baking sheet. Bake for 12 minutes.

Yields 32 cookies.

marbleized cookies

Quick, easy, and delicious!

3 cups flour
1½ cups margarine, plus 1 teaspoon
1½ cups sugar
1¼ teaspoons baking soda

1 egg, beaten
¼ cup chocolate chips
2 tablespoons water

Combine flour, 1½ cups margarine, sugar, baking soda, and egg. Melt chocolate chips and add 1 teaspoon margarine and water. Marbleize into dough. Form dough into 1-inch-thick logs. Wrap and freeze for about 1 hour until firm. Slice into ½-inch slices and place on a greased baking sheet. Bake in a preheated 350° oven until golden brown.

almond crescents

These crescents, dipped in melted chocolate, make the perfect addition to any dessert platter. They will virtually melt in your mouth.

1 cup margarine
2 teaspoons vanilla extract
1 cup powdered sugar
pinch of salt

¾ cup finely chopped almonds
2 cups flour
3 ounces bittersweet chocolate, melted

Cream together margarine, vanilla, and powdered sugar. Stir in salt, chopped almonds, and flour. Shape into balls or crescents. Bake in a preheated 350° oven for 15–18 minutes. Let cool and dip in melted chocolate.

Yields 5 dozen.

caramel-pecan cookies

*Adding pecans and chocolate icing turns a great cookie into a
fabulous one.*

½ cup margarine
½ cup brown sugar
1 egg
1 egg yolk
1 teaspoon vanilla extract
¼ teaspoon salt
¼ teaspoon baking soda
1½ cups flour

⅔ cup coarsely chopped or broken
  pecans

CHOCOLATE ICING
¼ cup cocoa
2 tablespoons margarine
2–3 tablespoons warm water
2 cups powdered sugar
1 teaspoon vanilla

Cream margarine and sugar. Beat in egg, egg yolk, and vanilla. Stir in
salt, baking soda, and flour. Add pecans last and mix well. Shape into
balls the size of a walnut and place on a lined cookie sheet. Bake for 12
minutes. Do not overbake.

For icing, beat all ingredients together with a mixer or by hand, until
smooth. Frost top of cooled cookies.

Yields 36 cookies.

pecan-topped cookies

This is an heirloom recipe that a friend brought with her from America upon making aliyah. These pecan-topped cookies are both crispy and delicious, as well as easy to prepare. You'll want to make them often.

1 cup margarine
½ cup brown sugar
½ cup white sugar
1 egg
1 teaspoon cinnamon

1 teaspoon almond extract
2½ cups flour
pecan halves or quarters, for top of cookies

Cream margarine with brown and white sugar. Beat in egg. Add cinnamon, almond extract, and flour. Pinch off pieces of dough and shape into balls with your hands. Place on a greased cookie sheet. Flatten slightly with the tines of a fork both ways. Place half pecan on top. Bake in a preheated 350° oven for about 12 minutes.

Yields 3½–4 dozen cookes.

mandelbrodt

Mandelbrodt (literally "almond bread") is an old European favorite and a traditional treat on Shabbos and holidays. This is an especially light recipe — absolutely delicious.

3 eggs
1 cup sugar
1 cup oil
1 teaspoon almond extract
¼ teaspoon salt
3 cups flour

2½ teaspoons baking powder
1 tablespoon vanilla extract
1 cup sliced almonds
⅓ cup sugar
2 teaspoons cinnamon

Beat eggs until light and fluffy. Beat in the sugar, oil, almond extract, salt, flour, baking powder, vanilla, and almonds. Shape into three long rolls. Place the rolls in a greased 11x17-inch jelly roll pan and bake in a preheated 350° oven for 35 minutes. In a small bowl, combine sugar and cinnamon. Cut mandelbrodt rolls into slices about 1-inch thick while still warm. Turn slices on side and sprinkle with sugar-cinnamon mixture. Return to oven for 15 more minutes.

Yields 36 slices.

VARIATION

Glorified Mandelbrodt: Divide dough into three sections. Roll each section into a rectangle. Spread with jam and sprinkle with coconut, nuts, and raisins. Roll up and place on a greased cookie sheet. Bake at 350° for 45 minutes or until golden brown. Let cool and slice.

Whole Wheat Mandelbrodt: Use 3 cups whole wheat flour in place of white flour, and 1 cup brown sugar in place of white sugar. Prepare with remaining ingredients and follow instructions above.

sufganiyot

Sufganiyot, or jelly doughnuts, are a popular Chanuka delicacy because they are deep fried in oil, and help us to remember the small vial of oil found in the Beis Hamikdash that lasted for eight days.

2 ounces yeast
1 cup sugar
2 cups water
7–7½ cups flour
½ cup oil
3 tablespoons cognac

2 teaspoons vanilla extract
2 eggs, beaten with a fork
1 tablespoon salt
oil, for frying
½ cup jam, for filling sufganiyot
powdered sugar, for sprinkling

In a large mixing bowl, dissolve yeast and 1 teaspoon sugar in ½ cup lukewarm water. Let stand for about 5 minutes until mixture becomes foamy. Add 6 cups flour to the bowl. Add remaining water, sugar, oil, cognac, vanilla, eggs, and salt. Mix on low speed for 3 minutes. Add remaining flour, then increase mixing speed to medium and mix for about 5 more minutes. Cover bowl with a dish towel and let rise for 1½ hours until double in bulk. Punch dough down. Divide dough into 4 parts. Roll each part into a ½-inch-thick rectangle. With a glass or large cookie cutter dipped in flour, cut into 3-inch rounds. Cover and let rise for 1 hour.

To fry, fill a pot 2–3 inches high with oil. Heat oil and carefully drop in several circles. Do not overcrowd. Fry for about 3 minutes on each side until golden brown and then place on a paper towel to drain excess oil. When cool, cut a small slit in the side and insert 1 teaspoon jam. Close tightly. Sprinkle with powdered sugar.

Yields 40 sufganiyot.

PASTRIES, PIES & CHEESECAKES

ROGELACH

My mother was a great balabusteh. Whatever she baked had "toisand ta'am." That's the expression Mama used with something she thought was simply delicious. Her rogelach (tiny cinnamon rolls) were special — literally mouth-watering. Once, when I visited her in her home in another city, I watched her roll out the dough and noticed how generously she smeared it with oil to enrich the flavor. At my request she wrote out her recipe, which I took with me back to Chicago.

A few days later, I decided to bake these rogelach. I took out Mama's recipe and prepared to bake. I looked at the recipe and noticed that the ingredients were listed, but the measurements were missing. In desperation I made that long distance phone call to her at home.

"Mama," I exclaimed, "how much sugar do you use in your rogelach?"

"Sugar? Not too much, don't make it too sweet. Use a bissel — just a little."

"And eggs, you forgot to write down how many eggs!"

"Eggs, well, ah, it depends how many you have in the house, three or four. If you're short you can put one less in."

I thought to myself, one less than what?

"And about the yeast, Mama, how much yeast does it take?"

"Oy," she exclaimed, anxiety rising in her voice. "Don't use too much yeast or it will make the cake dry. Just a small piece of yeast is all you need."

At this point I was even more confused. "What about the water? It doesn't say how much water."

"What's the matter with you, Sara?" Now, I could hear her getting upset with me. "Don't you know how much water to use? Viffel es fanemt — as much as it takes."

I could hear her continuing, "And don't let the dough rise all over your kitchen, otherwise it will taste yeasty. Dough needs care like a baby. You can cover it and put it to rest for a couple of hours until it is double, but don't think you can spend the morning shopping or visiting your friends and forget about it."

(The exact details of this conversation are a product of my imagination!)

Don't worry, I won't pass on Mama's original recipe to you. You get tried-and-true recipes with measurements.

rogelach

A dainty version of classic rogelach with a rich flavor. In our home we make these delectables for special occasions and vary the size of the rogelach based on the crowd.

DOUGH

2 cups margarine

⅔ cup sugar

4 eggs

½ cup lukewarm water

2 teaspoons vanilla extract

2 packages (2½ tablespoons) dry yeast

6 cups flour

½ teaspoon salt

apricot jam, for spreading on dough

FILLING

1 cup sugar

½ cup cocoa

1 teaspoon cinnamon

1 cup chopped nuts

Cream margarine and sugar. Beat in eggs and then add remaining dough ingredients. Divide into 5 balls about 1½-inches in diameter. Roll out each ball into an 8-inch circle. Spread apricot jam on top. Combine filling ingredients and sprinkle generously over dough. Cut into 8 pie-shaped wedges. Roll up each wedge, starting at wide end. Place on a greased cookie sheet. Do not let rise. Bake in a preheated 350° oven until golden brown.

Yields 40 rogelach.

TIP

A few drops of yellow coloring in the dough will give yeast cake a more professional look.

special rogelach

These incredible rogelach will literally melt in your mouth.

1 cup margarine

5 cups flour

½ cup sugar

¼ teaspoon salt

1 8-ounce carton whipped topping

oil, for spreading on dough

powdered sugar, for dipping

melted chocolate, for drizzling on top, optional

With a pastry cutter or two table knives, cut margarine into flour until it resembles peas, or mix in electric mixer, starting on low speed, until it resembles cornmeal. Mix in sugar, salt, and dessert topping until smooth. Refrigerate for one or two hours for easier handling. Divide into 2–2½-inch balls. Roll out each ball into 7–8-inch thin rounds. Spread with a little oil. Combine ingredients of chocolate or cinnamon filling and sprinkle on each circle. Cut into six wedge-shaped slices. Roll up, starting from wide end, and bend ends inward slightly to form crescent. Place on a greased cookie sheet and bake in a preheated 350° oven until golden brown. Remove from oven and roll in powdered sugar or drizzle melted chocolate on top.

If desired, roll out into smaller circles for miniature rogelach.

CHOCOLATE FILLING

1 cup granulated sugar

1 cup powdered sugar

2½ teaspoons vanilla sugar

1 cup cocoa

CINNAMON FILLING

2 teaspoons cinnamon

1½ cups granulated sugar

TIP

When measuring cups of powdered ingredients, such as cocoa or flour, gently spoon ingredients into the cup with a tablespoon and level it off.

schnecken

Schnecken are little individual cinnamon rolls which can be made in muffin pans, either large or miniature size.

DOUGH
1 recipe Classic Yeast Dough, or
    Refrigerator Coffee Cake Dough
oil, for smearing on dough

FILLING
1 cup sugar
1 tablespoon cinnamon

⅔ cup chopped nuts
½ cup raisins

SUGAR-NUT MIXTURE
oil
1 cup brown sugar
1 cup pecan halves

Follow instructions for preparing yeast dough. Once the dough has risen, divide it in 2 or 3 parts. Roll each part out to ¼ inch thickness in rectangle shape. Smear oil generously on top. Mix together sugar and cinnamon and sprinkle on top. Then sprinkle with nuts and raisins. Roll as for jelly roll.

Cut cinnamon roll into 1½ inch thick slices. Line muffin pan with paper cupcake holders. Place a teaspoon of oil into each place. Put in 2 or 3 half-pecans and then 1 or 2 teaspoons sugar into each place. Place one slice of raw cinnamon roll in each muffin place on top of the oil-sugar-nut mixture. Cover and let stand for about 30 minutes. Bake 20–25 minutes in a 375° oven.

Yields 36 schnecken.

VARIATION

Schnecken with Chocolate Filling: Follow directions for cocoa filling for yeast dough.

refrigerator coffee cake dough

Known as "cold yeast dough," this dough can be prepared the night before, left to rise in the refrigerator, and used the following morning.

2 tablespoons dry yeast
2 teaspoons, plus ⅓ cup sugar
¾ cup lukewarm water
1 cup margarine
1 egg

1 egg yolk
2 tablespoons whiskey
1½ teaspoons salt
4 cups flour
2 tablespoons oil, for spreading on dough

In a mixer bowl, dissolve yeast and 2 teaspoons sugar in water. Cover and let stand 10 minutes until bubbly. Add margarine, remaining sugar, egg, egg yolk, whiskey, salt, and flour. Beat at medium speed until smooth. Beat for an additional 5 minutes. Place dough in a greased bowl. Turn over, cover with a cloth, and refrigerate several hours or overnight. Punch down. Leave at room temperature for ½ an hour before filling. Roll out dough and spread with oil. Spread with filling (see below). Roll as for a jelly roll and bake in a preheated 375° oven for 30–35 minutes until golden brown.

RAISIN-NUT FILLING
1 cup sugar
1 tablespoon cocoa
⅔ cup chopped nuts
½ cup raisins
grated rind of 1 lemon
1 teaspoon cinnamon

Combine all ingredients and sprinkle over dough.

ORANGE FILLING
⅔ cup margarine
2 tablespoons grated orange peel
4 tablespoons orange juice
3 cups powdered sugar

Beat together in an electric mixer until creamy and spread on rolled-out dough.

baklava

A rich Middle Eastern pastry.

1 cup olive oil or canola oil
1 pound package phylo dough

NUT FILLING
2½ cups coarsely chopped walnuts,
    almonds, or pecans
4 tablespoons powdered sugar

HONEY SYRUP
1 cup honey
2 cups sugar
1¾ cups hot water
juice of 1 lemon
½ teaspoon cinnamon

Brush each sheet of phyllo dough with oil. Place half of the package of oiled sheets in a greased 9-inch square baking pan. Combine chopped nuts and sugar for filling and spread evenly over the top of phyllo dough in the pan. Add the remaining sheets of phyllo dough, one layer at a time, covering each sheet with a layer of filling. End with a sheet of phyllo dough on top. Brush with oil. With a sharp knife, mark pieces by cutting the top into squares or diamond shapes. Tuck in the ends. Bake in a preheated 375° oven for 40 minutes until golden brown.

Combine ingredients for honey syrup, except for the lemon juice, and simmer on low fire for about 10 minutes. Add lemon juice. Remove Baklava from the oven and cut the marked dough through the layers. While still hot, pour syrup over top. Cool and serve.

Yields 30 pieces.

hamantaschen

Hamantaschen (literally, "Haman's Pockets") are an age-old pastry that remind us of the Purim miracle. My family makes this recipe year after year on Purim and it consistently yields fantastic results.

½ cup margarine
⅔ cup sugar
1 teaspoon vanilla extract
2 eggs

2½ cups flour (part whole wheat
    flour may be used)
2 teaspoons baking powder
pinch of salt

Cream together margarine, sugar, and vanilla. Stir in eggs. Blend in flour, baking powder, and salt. Divide dough in half and place in a plastic bag. Refrigerate for a few hours. When ready to bake, roll each half of dough to ⅛-inch thickness. With a 3-inch cookie cutter, or the rim of a water glass, cut out circles of dough. Alternatively, cut into 2½ inch squares. Place a teaspoonful of filling in center of each circle. Pinch the edges tightly together, forming a triangle. Leave a little of the filling showing in the center. Place on a greased baking sheet and bake in a preheated 350° oven for 15–20 minutes until golden brown.

Yields about 2 dozen Hamantaschen.

POPPY SEED FILLING

1 cup ground poppy seeds
½ cup honey
⅓ cup raisins

juice of ½ a lemon
1 tablespoon oil

Combine all ingredients and spoon onto dough circles.

DATE FILLING

¼ cup margarine or oil
⅓ cup brown sugar
1½ cups chopped dates

½ teaspoon cinnamon
¼ teaspoon ginger
grated rind of 1 lemon

Melt margarine over a low flame (or heat oil) and stir in sugar and dates. Simmer on low heat for 5 minutes. Remove from heat. Add cinnamon, ginger, and grated lemon rind and mix well. Spoon onto dough circles.

cheese knishes

A welcome change from potato knishes, these knishes make a great addition to a milchig buffet and are perfect for noshing any time.

DOUGH

½ cup margarine

3 cups flour

1 cup sour cream, leben, or plain yogurt

FILLING

2 pounds dry cottage cheese or farmer cheese

2 eggs, beaten

⅓–½ cup sugar, or to taste

¼ teaspoon salt

½ cup raisins, soaked in hot water for 10 minutes

½ teaspoon cinnamon

GLAZE

1 egg yolk, beaten with 2 teaspoons water

With two table knives or a pastry cutter, cut margarine into flour. Stir in sour cream, leben, or yogurt. Knead for a few minutes or mix in electric mixer. Put in a plastic bag and refrigerate 2–3 hours.

Divide dough into 4 parts. Roll each part into a rectangle. Mix together ingredients for filling, and spread onto dough. Roll as for jelly roll. Brush with glaze. Place on a greased baking sheet. Cut ⅔ of the way through at 2-inch intervals. Bake in a preheated 350° oven for 40 minutes. Cut through after baking.

Yields 30–40 slices.

aunt gertie's cheese strudel

My Aunt Gertie made this cheese strudel over fifty years ago, and already then it was a family favorite. Her daughter Miryam lives in Talpiot, Jerusalem and still enjoys making this recipe, especially on Shavuos and Chanuka.

DOUGH
1 cup margarine
1 cup plain yogurt
2½ cups flour
1 teaspoon baking powder
generous pinch of salt
oil, for spreading on dough

FILLING
2 pounds farmer cheese or dry
   cottage cheese
3 eggs
⅓ cup sugar, to taste
½ cup raisins, soaked in hot water
   for 10 minutes

Cream margarine and yogurt. Stir in flour, baking powder, and salt. Divide into 5 balls. In a separate bowl, combine ingredients for filling. Roll out one part of dough and spread with oil. Place ⅕ of cheese mixture along inside edge of dough. Roll. Place roll on a greased baking sheet. With a sharp knife, cut at 1½-inch intervals, halfway down, to mark the slices and to keep the dough from puffing up. Repeat with remaining pieces of dough. Bake in a preheated 350° oven for 40–45 minutes.

Yields 50 slices.

TIP

When doubling a recipe, do not double the salt.
Just add a pinch more.

chocolate strudel

The ultimate chocolate strudel: A rich dough containing whipped topping, filled with a moist chocolate mixture, then sprinkled with powdered sugar and drizzled with melted chocolate.

DOUGH

1 8-ounce container whipped topping
6 cups flour
2 cups margarine
2 teaspoons vanilla extract

3 eggs
½ cup cocoa
¼ cup oil
1 teaspoon baking powder
1 cup flour
2 teaspoons vanilla extract

FILLING

1 cup margarine
1½ cups sugar

TOPPING

powdered sugar
chocolate, melted

Mix together all ingredients for dough. Divide into 5 parts. Prepare filling: Cream margarine and sugar. Beat in eggs. Add remaining ingredients and mix until smooth. Roll each piece of dough into a rectangle. Spoon some of filling along center length of rolled-out dough. Fold dough over from both sides. Tuck ends in. Place on a lined cookie sheet with seams down. With a sharp knife, cut at 1½-inch intervals, halfway down, to prevent dough from puffing up. Bake in a preheated 375° oven for about 25 minutes until golden brown. Sprinkle top of each roll with powdered sugar and drizzle melted chocolate on top.

Yields 60 slices.

TIP

To make your own powdered sugar, put 1 cup of granulated sugar with 1 tablespoon cornstarch in the food processor and process for about 2 minutes.

leah's food processor strudel dough

For those who like using the food-processor, a dough that is simple to prepare, and even simpler to clean up.

3 cups flour
2 teaspoons baking powder
1 cup oil

1 cup hot water
½ teaspoon salt
oil, for brushing on top

Combine all ingredients in a food processor and process until smooth. Do not overmix. Let rest 10 minutes. Divide into 2 or 3 parts. Roll out each part into a rectangle. Brush dough generously with oil. Spread with filling and bake as directed in a preheated 350° oven until golden brown.

raspberry-nut strudel

Try this sweet and delicious strudel, made with raspberry jam.

1 recipe strudel dough or 1 2-pound
    package of puff pastry
oil for spreading on dough
½ cup bread crumbs

FILLING
1 cup raspberry preserves

1 cup coarsely chopped walnuts
1 cup raisins
1 cup shredded coconut, optional
½ teaspoon cinnamon
½ cup bread crumbs

Combine raspberry preserves, chopped walnuts, raisins, coconut, and cinnamon. Roll out pastry dough very thin (do not divide). Spread with oil, then sprinkle with bread crumbs. Spread with preserves and nut mixture. Roll as for jelly roll. Place on lined cookie sheet in a U shape. Brush oil over top and sides of roll. Cut ¾ of the way down at 1½-inch intervals. Bake in a preheated 450° oven for 20 minutes. Reduce heat to 350° and continue baking for additional 20 minutes until golden brown.

Yields 24 slices.

apricot-nut strudel

*A decadent dough that makes the perfect dessert
for your milchig occasion.*

DOUGH
8 ounces cream cheese
1 cup margarine or butter
3 cups flour

FILLING
1 12-ounce jar apricot jam
1 cup chopped nuts

1 cup shredded coconut
1 cup raisins
½ cup sugar
1 teaspoon cinnamon
⅔ cup cookie crumbs or bread crumbs

Mix together cream cheese, margarine or butter, and flour. Divide into 3 parts. Refrigerate 1 hour or overnight. Combine ingredients for filling. Roll out dough into rectangles and spread with filling. Roll as for jelly roll. Place on lined cookie sheet and bake in a preheated 350° oven for 30 minutes or until golden brown.

Yields 36 slices.

TIP

To tint coconut, put a small amount of shredded coconut in a glass jar. Add a few drops of food coloring, cover the jar, and shake until the coconut is colored.

cabbage strudel

A time-honored recipe, cabbage strudel is served alongside the main dish, rather than as a dessert. My mother used to make this recipe for special yom tov meals.

1 2-pound package puff pastry dough

FILLING

1 16-ounce package shredded cabbage

4 tablespoons olive oil

½ cup brown sugar, packed

1 cup raisins or currants

½ cup coarsely chopped almonds, optional

½ teaspoon salt

3 tablespoons bread crumbs

juice of ½ a lemon

1 teaspoon cinnamon

GLAZE

1 egg yolk, beaten with 1 teaspoon water

Sauté cabbage in oil, stirring frequently for about 30 minutes. Stir in remaining filling ingredients and continue cooking 10 more minutes. Let cool. Meanwhile, divide puff pastry dough into 2 or 3 sections and roll out.

Spread cabbage mixture along inside edge of rolled-out dough. Roll as for jelly roll and place on a greased 11x17-inch cookie sheet. Brush top with glaze. Mark slices by cutting halfway down rolls at 1–1½ inch intervals. Bake in a preheated 425° oven for 20 minutes. Lower heat to 350° and continue baking 10–15 minutes more, until golden brown.

Yields 24 slices.

T I P

When baking pastries using flaky dough, start in a very hot oven (425°) for 15-20 minutes, then reduce heat to 350°-375° for the rest of the baking time.

spinach strudel

*Spinach strudel is an unusual and different milchige side dish.
It has far less calories than a dessert strudel, because it is made
without sugar or jam, and the spinach and cheese filling makes it a
healthful addition to any meal.*

1 recipe strudel dough or 1 2-pound
    package puff pastry dough

3 teaspoons oil

FILLING

2 10-ounce packages frozen spin-
    ach, thawed and drained

1½ cups grated Parmesan cheese

¼ cup oil

1 medium onion, diced

salt and pepper, to taste

½ cup bread crumbs

Combine spinach with cheese, oil, onion, salt, and pepper. Mix well.
Divide strudel dough or puff pastry dough into 3 pieces, and roll out
1 piece into a rectangle. Brush with 1 teaspoon oil, then sprinkle with
bread crumbs. Place a third of spinach mixture in a row along inside
edge of the rolled-out dough. Roll as for a jelly roll. Place on a greased
cookie sheet, seam side down. Brush with a little oil. Repeat for other
two rolls. Bake in a preheated 425° oven for 20 minutes. Lower heat
to 350° and continue baking about 15 minutes more, until golden
brown.

Yields 30–26 slices.

cherry crumb pie

This double-crumbed pie is a Friday-night special in our home. It is also very easy to prepare, since the cherry in the filling comes right out of a can.

CRUMB MIXTURE
3 cups flour
1 teaspoon baking powder
¾ cup sugar
1 egg
¾ cup oil

pinch of salt
1 teaspoon vanilla extract

FILLING
1 can cherry pie filling
5 large grand apples, peeled and
     thinly sliced

Mix together all ingredients for crumb mixture. Sprinkle ½ of mixture on bottom of a greased 9- or 10-inch pie pan. Place apples on top, and cover with cherry pie filling. Sprinkle remaining ½ of crumbs on top of cherry pie filling. Bake in a preheated 350° oven for 40–45 minutes.

Serves 8–10.

miri's fabulous cheesecake

Before each holiday I received this special cheesecake from my friend Miri as a token of our friendship. This is a large, delicious cheesecake that you'll love, with a topping that includes instant vanilla pudding for an especially rich flavor.

CRUST

1 cup margarine

1 cup sugar

3 eggs

2½ cups flour

3 teaspoons baking powder

FILLING

6 eggs, separated

3 8-ounce containers cream cheese

1 cup sugar

½ cup milk

1 tablespoon vanilla extract

½ cup instant vanilla pudding mix

1 cup plain yogurt or sour cream

½ cup flour

TOPPING

1 8-ounce container whipped topping

3 tablespoons instant vanilla pudding

To make the crust, cream margarine and sugar. Add eggs and beat well. Blend in flour and baking powder. Roll out dough and spread into a lined 11x14-inch baking pan. Beat egg yolks for filling until light. Add cream cheese, sugar, milk, vanilla, pudding mix, sour cream or yogurt, and flour. Beat egg whites until stiff and fold into mixture. Pour mixture onto dough in pan. Bake in a preheated 400° oven for 15 minutes. Reduce heat and continue baking at 350° for 40 minutes. To make topping, whip topping and fold in instant vanilla pudding mix. Spread over top of cake when finished baking.

Serves 24–30.

chocolate and white cream cheesecake

This is a cake for those who want to make traditional food with a gourmet touch. Two layers of smooth filling topped with cream, garnished with chocolate curls, it's a feast for the eyes and stomach.

CRUST
¾ cup chocolate cookie crumbs
¼ cup margarine, melted
3 tablespoons sugar

FILLING
1½ pounds cream cheese
1 cup sugar
5 eggs
1 teaspoon vanilla extract

4 ounces milk or dark chocolate, melted
2 tablespoons lemon juice

TOPPING (OPTIONAL)
8-ounce container whipping cream
2 tablespoons powdered sugar
½ teaspoon vanilla extract
chocolate curls, for garnish

Combine cookie crumbs, margarine, and sugar for crust and pat into a 10-inch baking pan. In an electric mixer, combine cream cheese and sugar for filling. Beat in eggs, one at a time. Add vanilla. Remove 2 cups of mixture and stir into it melted chocolate. Add lemon juice to remaining cheese mixture. Pour white mixture onto crust. Pour chocolate mixture on top. Bake in a preheated 350° oven for 40–45 minutes. Let cool. If desired, make topping by whipping cream with powdered sugar and vanilla. Spread on top of cooled cheesecake and garnish with chocolate curls.

VARIATION

Chocolate Swirl Cheesecake: Add melted chocolate to only ½ cup of cheese mixture. Pour white mixture into cookie crumb crust and drop tablespoons of chocolate mixture on top. Swirl by running a knife back and forth through the cheesecake before baking.

no-bake chocolate cheesecake

If you don't have a milchig oven,
this cheesecake is an excellent choice.

CRUST

1½ cups chocolate cookie crumbs

⅓ cup margarine, melted

FILLING

8 ounces white cheese

½ cup sugar

2 teaspoons vanilla extract

2 eggs, separated

6 ounces semi-sweet chocolate, melted

1 8-ounce container whipping cream, whipped

½–⅔ cup chopped walnuts

For crust: Mix together cookie crumbs and margarine. Press into a 9-inch springform pan. Bake in a preheated 325° oven for 10 minutes. Combine white cheese, ¼ cup sugar, and vanilla. Stir in beaten egg yolks and melted chocolate. In another bowl, beat egg whites, gradually adding remaining ¼ cup sugar, until stiff. Fold stiffly beaten egg whites into chocolate mixture. Fold in whipped cream and nuts. Pour mixure into cookie crust. If desired, top with additional whipped cream.

Serves 8–10.

fantastic cheesecake

A neighbor who hails from London brought over this cheesecake
erev Shavuos. After tasting just a bit, I knew this was a recipe that
had to be shared. Note: Only the crust is baked.

CRUST
¾ cup margarine
5 tablespoons sugar
1 egg
2 cups flour
2 teaspoons baking powder
¼ teaspoon salt

FILLING
3 8-ounce containers white cheese
¾ cup sugar
2 tablespoons instant vanilla pudding mix, or 2 teaspoons vanilla extract
1 8-ounce container whipped topping

Cream margarine and sugar. Beat in egg. Stir in flour, baking powder, and salt. Pat ¾ of dough into bottom of a greased 9-inch pie pan. Flatten remaining ¼ of dough onto greased silver foil or a small pan. Bake in a preheated 350° oven for 30 minutes.

Combine white cheese, sugar, and vanilla pudding mix. Pour onto baked crust. Beat whipped topping until fluffy and spread over cheese mixture. Crumble small pieces of crust and sprinkle on top. Refrigerate.

Serves 8–10.

TIP

To keep pie dough tender and prevent it from
shrinking during baking, refrigerate the
wrapped dough for several hours or overnight.
Remove the dough from refrigerator about half
an hour before shaping.

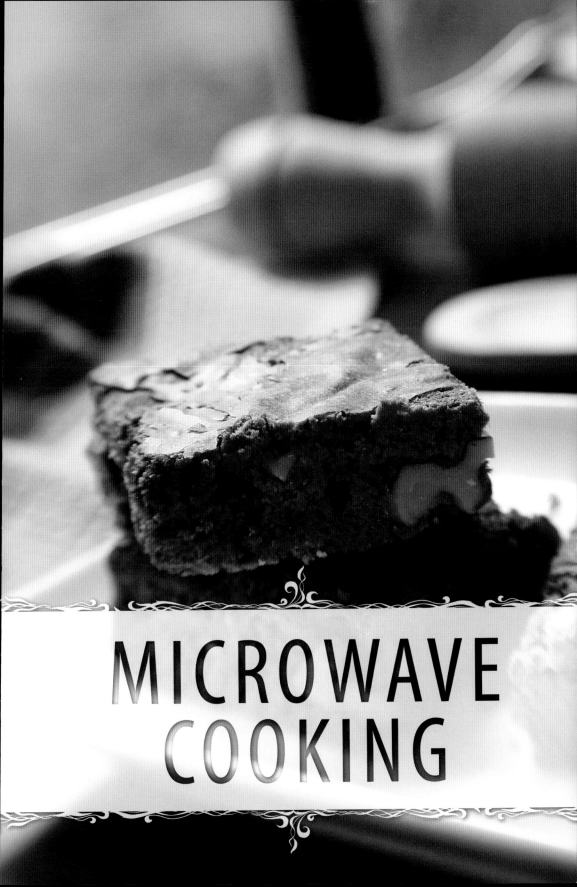

MICROWAVE COOKING

MICROWAVE COOKING

I visited a friend one afternoon and found her looking harried and upset. "What's bothering you, Ahuva?" I asked.

"My microwave is at the repair shop and I have some yeshivah bachurim dropping in today. When they come, I usually take food from the freezer and heat it in the microwave. You know," she went on, "I think I have to have two microwave ovens. I just can't be without one."

Well, I thought, that's really going too far — unless, of course, she uses one for fleishig and one for milchig.

The good news is that reheating food in a microwave helps the food retain more nutrients than it would if kept hot for a long time in a regular oven.

Cooking food in a minimal amount of water for reduced time — as occurs with microwaving — ensures the retention of certain vitamins, particulalry vitamin C and thiamin. Microwave cooking is more similar to steaming than to boiling, and minimizes the leaking of vitamins and minerals into the cooking water.

Cooking food in the microwave does not present a risk of radiation. Microwaves stop as soon as the power is switched off. Food cooked in a microwave is healthy and wholesome. However, food cooked in a microwave does not heat uniformly, which may cause portions of the food to be undercooked or inadequately heated. Though fans and turntables help to alleviate this problem, it is still recommended to stir the food part way through cooking. Those dishes such as laasagne that cannot be stirrred should be allowed to stand at least five minutes to reach a uniform temperature.

Frozen food should be completely thawed before microwaving, since incomplete thawing causes uneven cooking. When cooking or heating large quantities of food, divide the food into smaller portions.

Remember with a microwave you can have a hot mealt to serve your family in a quarter of the time it would take to prepare in a regular oven.

microwave fish

A quick and easy way to prepare baked fish.

4 slices of fish (whitefish, trout, salmon, or halibut)

salt, to taste

garlic powder, for sprinkling

paprika, for sprinkling

lemon wedges, for garnish

Sprinkle fish lightly with salt on all sides. Sprinkle with garlic powder and paprika. Refrigerate for about ½ hour. Cover and microwave on high for 8–9 minutes. Let stand covered for 5 minutes. Serve warm, garnished with lemon wedges dipped in paprika.

Serves 4.

VARIATION

Microwave Fish with Diced Tomato: Combine 2 large diced tomatoes with 1 small chopped onion. Stir in salt, pepper, and garlic powder to taste, 1 tablespoon olive oil, and 2 tablespoons water. Place in a microwave-safe baking dish. Cover and microwave on high for 5 minutes. Place the 4 slices of seasoned raw fish on top. Cover. Return to oven and microwave on high for an additional 9 minutes.

(M)

microwave baked chicken

An amazing fleishig meal for those days when you're short on time.

1 3-pound chicken, cut in eighths
½ teaspoon garlic powder
⅔ teaspoon paprika
¼ teaspoon pepper

⅓ cup honey
2 tablespoons mustard
1 4-ounce can sliced mushrooms,
   drained

Combine garlic powder, paprika, and pepper and rub over chicken pieces. Combine honey and mustard in a small bowl and spread on chicken.
Place chicken in microwave-safe dish or Pyrex dish. Scatter sliced mushrooms on top. Cover and microwave on high for 12-13 minutes. Let
stand covered for about 5 minutes. If desired, brown under broiler or in
oven before serving.

Serves 4–6.

=== T I P ===

*For a beautiful garnish, sprinkle coarsely
chopped parsley or dill, or chopped green
onions, on boiled potatoes before serving.*

Ⓜ

microwave meatballs with spaghetti and tomato sauce

Try this "see–it–and–believe–it" recipe yourself and discover that meatballs and spaghetti can be made in no time.

1 pound ground beef
1 large egg, beaten
¼ cup bread crumbs

1 small onion, diced
½ cup water
¼ teaspoon pepper

Combine all ingredients for meatballs and shape into balls the size of walnuts. Place in a microwave-safe pan or Pyrex dish. Cover with baking paper. Microwave on high for 5-6 minutes. Drain and serve with spaghetti and tomato sauce.

Serves 4–5.

TOMATO SAUCE

1 large onion, diced
2 cloves garlic, minced
2 tablespoons vegetable oil
2 large tomatoes, diced
2 tablespoons tomato sauce

½ cup water
½ teaspoon salt
¼ teaspoon pepper
2 tablespoons sugar
2 teaspoons cornstarch

Microwave chopped onion and garlic in oil for 3 minutes until tender. Add tomatoes, tomato sauce, water, salt, pepper, and sugar. Cook uncovered on high for 5 minutes. Stir in cornstarch and microwave on high for 3 minutes until thickened. Remove from microwave and puree with hand blender or in food processor until smooth.

microwave vegetable lasagna

I innovated this microwave lasagna at a time when I didn't have a milchig oven. It tastes terrific — my family loves it!

1 10-ounce package frozen chopped broccoli, thawed

1 egg, beaten

1 cup cottage cheese

½ teaspoon salt

¼ teaspoon pepper

4 ounces shredded mozzzarella cheese

4 ounces medium whole wheat lasagna noodles, cooked

½ cup shredded Parmesan cheese

SAUCE

1 large onion, diced

2 tablespoons oil

1¼ cups tomato sauce

1¼–1½ cups water

2 cloves garlic, minced

½ teaspoon salt

¼ teaspoon pepper

3½ tablespoons sugar

½ teaspoon oregano

Cook broccoli for 10 minutes until nearly tender. In a bowl, combine egg, cottage cheese, cooked broccoli, salt, pepper, and cheese. Set aside. For the sauce: Sauté the onion in oil and combine with remaining sauce ingredients. In a Pyrex pan, spread a layer of lasagna noodles, a layer of sauce, and a layer of cheese mixture. Repeat layering, ending with noodles and the remaining tomato sauce. Sprinkle with shredded Parmesan cheese. Cover and microwave on high for 20 minutes. Let stand in microwave for 5 minutes. Remove and let stand 5 minutes more before serving.

Serves 5–6.

VARIATION

Mushroom or Spinach Lasagna: Omit broccoli. Add a 4-ounce can sliced mushrooms, drained, or ½ pound fresh mushrooms, sliced and sautéed; or 10 ounces fresh chopped spinach, cooked and drained.

long-grain rice

It doesn't get easier than this!

2 cups water
1 teaspoon salt

1 tablespoon oil
1 cup long-grain rice

Combine water, salt, and oil in a large microwave-safe pan. Microwave on high until water is boiling. Stir in rice. Cover and microwave on high for 15-16 minutes. Let stand for 5 minutes. Fluff with fork.

Serves 3–4.

stuffed potatoes

The simple baked potato turned into an elegant party dish.

4 medium baking potatoes
3 ounces cream cheese
1–2 scallions, thinly sliced
½ cup plain yogurt
2 tablespoons olive oil

¼ teaspoon garlic powder
salt and pepper, to taste
paprika, for sprinkling on top
parsley, for sprinkling on top

Prick potatoes in a few places with a fork. Cover and bake on high for about 16 minutes. Slice off the top of each potato and carefully scoop out the inside, leaving a ½ inch shell intact. Place in a bowl and mash. Stir in cream cheese, sliced scallions, yogurt, olive oil, garlic powder, salt, and pepper. Return mixture to shells. Sprinkle paprika and parsley on top. Return to microwave and heat on full power for about 3 minutes.

Serves 4.

VARIATION

Sprinkle top of potatoes with shredded yellow cheese, and microwave for 1 minute until cheese is melted.

onion pashtida

A quick, delicious, quiche-like dish — without the crust.

4 eggs	¼ teaspoon pepper
½ cup canola oil	5 medium onions, diced
¼ cup water	¾ cup flour
1½ teaspoons salt	1 teaspoon baking powder

Beat eggs well. Stir in oil, water, salt, pepper, and onions. Blend in flour and baking powder. Pour into a greased 8x10-inch Pyrex dish or microwave-safe pan. Microwave on high for 13–14 minutes. If desired, to brown top, place baked pashtida under broiler for several minutes, or in a preheated 400° oven for 10 minutes. This can also be baked in a regular oven at 350° for about 50 minutes until golden brown.

Serves 8–10.

VARIATION:

Milchig Onion Pashtida: Sprinkle ½ cup shredded cheddar or American cheese on top before baking.

TIP

*Cover microwaved food with paper towels
to avoid splattering.*

microwave ratatouille

An old French relish adapted for the microwave.

1 large eggplant, peeled and cut
    into small cubes
1 large onion, diced
2 cloves garlic, minced
3 tablespoons olive oil
1 green pepper, cut into strips

2 zucchini, thinly sliced
3 tomatoes, peeled and diced
salt, to taste
generous pinch of pepper
3–4 tablespoons tomato sauce,
    optional

In a 2-quart casserole, combine eggplant, onion, garlic, and oil. Cover and microwave on high for 3 minutes. Stir and return to microwave for 3 more minutes. Place a layer of green pepper strips on top, followed by a layer of zucchini and then a layer of tomatoes. Add salt and pepper, and tomato sauce, if desired. Stir. Cover and microwave on high for about 10 minutes until vegetables are tender. Let stand covered for 5 minutes.

Serves 4–6.

microwave applesauce

Delicious and yet so simple to prepare! Make a large quantity to store in your freezer until you are ready to serve it.

6–8 tart apples, peeled, cored, and sliced
3 tablespoons water
1 tablespoon fresh lemon juice
¼ cup brown or white sugar
1 teaspoon cinnamon
pinch of salt
¼ teaspoon nutmeg, optional
2–3 tablespoons jam, optional

Place all ingredients in a Pyrex or microwave baking dish. Cover and microwave for 5-6 minutes on high until apples are soft. Mash or purée with a hand blender. If desired, leave some pieces of apple unpuréed.

Serves 4–6.

microwave strawberry sauce

A terrific ice cream topping perfect for those hot summer days when you don't want to turn on the stove.

1 teaspoon cornstarch
1 tablespoon cold water
½ cup sugar
¾ pound fresh or frozen strawberries, hulled and sliced
½ cup orange juice

Dissolve cornstarch in water. Add sugar. Stir in strawberries. Microwave on high for 2 minutes or until thickened. Stir halfway through cooking time. Add orange juice and microwave an additional 1½ minutes until warm.

Yields about 2 cups.

microwave brownies

A boon for the housewife in a hurry.

1 cup sugar
2 eggs
⅓ cup oil
2 ounces unsweetened chocolate,
    melted

1 teaspoon vanilla
½ cup coarsely chopped nuts
¾ cup sifted flour
½ teaspoon baking powder
¼ teaspoon salt

In a mixing bowl mix together the sugar and eggs. Stir in the oil, melted chocolate, vanilla, and nuts. Add the flour, baking powder, and salt. Spread evenly in greased 8x8x2-inch Pyrex or other microwave-safe dish. Microwave on high for 8 minutes. Remove from microwave and cut into squares.

Yields 25 squares.

butterscotch marble squares

Baking these munchies is a terrific activity for kids, and everyone enjoys the butterscotch taste. They are also terrific midnight snacks.

½ cup margarine
1 cup brown sugar
1 egg
1 teaspoon vanilla extract
1 cup flour

½ teaspoon baking powder
⅛ teaspoon baking soda
generous pinch of salt
½ cup semi-sweet chocolate chips, melted

Cream margarine, brown sugar, egg, and vanilla. Stir in the flour, baking powder, baking soda, and salt. Mix until smooth. Spread mixture into an 8-inch square Pyrex baking pan. Pour melted chocolate on top and marbleize with a knife. Microwave on high for 5–5½ minutes until top springs back when pressed with finger.

Serves 12.

microwave cheesecake

Why wait till Shavuos to make cheesecake when you have a recipe that is so marvelously simple?

CRUMB CRUST

1½ cups cookie or tea biscuit
    crumbs

¼ cup oil

2 tablespoons brown sugar

½ teaspoon cinnamon

CHEESE FILLING

3 8-ounce containers cream cheese

1 cup sour cream or plain yogurt

2 eggs, beaten

1 teaspoon vanilla extract

1 tablespoon lemon juice

½–¾ cup sugar or Splenda

3 tablespoons flour

½ cup instant vanilla pudding mix,
    optional

TOPPING

1 cup sour cream or plain yogurt

2 tablespoons sugar

To make crust, mix together cookie crumbs and oil. Spread evenly in a 9-inch round or 7x11-inch Pyrex dish, coming up the sides a bit. Refrigerate or freeze for 1 hour to set. Mix all ingredients for filling together thoroughly and pour into prepared shell. Microwave on high for 10 minutes. Let stand 10 minutes to cool slightly. Combine sour cream or yogurt with sugar and spread over baked cheesecake. Return to microwave and bake on high for an additional 2 minutes. Let cool. Keep refrigerated until ready to serve.

Serves 8–10.

TIP

Wash your microwave regularly with detergent and warm water, using a soft cloth.

microwave frozen vegetables

*Vegetables should be covered with a standard microwave cover or a
paper bag with a slit on top so the steam can escape.*

Add 2 tablespoons water, salt and pepper to taste, and 1 tablespoon
vegetable oil or butter to the vegetables.

Asparagus spears	6–7 minutes
Broccoli florettes	6–7 minutes
Baby carrots	7 minutes
Cauliflower florets	5 minutes
Corn on the cob	
1 ear:	4½ minutes
2 ears:	6 minutes
4 ears:	11 minutes
Whole kernel corn	5 minutes
Green beans	6–7 minutes
Mixed vegetables	5–5½ minutes
Peas	3½ minutes
Peas and carrots	4–5 minutes
Spinach, chopped	5–5½ minutes

PESACH

PESACH IN THE 30'S

I have often wondered how my Aunt Esther, who lived with her family in Jerusalem about seven or eight decades ago, managed to prepare for Pesach, not only for her family but for the countless guests who came from many miles around.

There were no refrigerators, gas ranges, or freezers, not to mention food processors, blenders, or electric mixers. No one even knew the meaning of the word microwave oven, nor could they in their wildest imagination dream of either an electric dishwasher or a clothes dryer. Laundry was done in a washtub in the yard over a scrub board. In order for the family to have clean clothing and clean tablecloths to last the entire holiday it had to be done mamash on the day before Pesach. My aunt told me about the excitement it caused one year when just as the wash was completed and ready to be hung out, it rained, and the laundry had to remain in the tub until after yom tov.

Cooking was done on a campfire burner with a strong flame, called a "premus," where the pot of food was brought to a boil, and then transferred to a double-wick burner, called a "petilia," where the food was left to simmer until it was completely cooked.

Staples were scarce and rations were meager. Fish was considered a luxury, and the lowly potato was expensive. Potatoes were grated, drained, and dried and made into potato starch. It was a special treat for a family to get an apple or even an orange. Few vegetables were around — eggplant, squash, and maybe some tomatoes — they were all prepared in many different ways to provide variety to meals and sometimes to replace chicken or fish.

Serious preparations for Pesach began with the approach of the Sukkos season when plump, juicy grapes ripened. Because wine was not yet commercially produced, it was made by almost every household. With feet scrubbed clean, everyone, including the children, happily trampled the juice from the grapes. Sugar was added and the whole lot was poured into barrels to ferment. The results were sweet red wine, white wine, and grape juice with a delicious flavor.

Oranges ripened Chanukah time and the housewife got busy making orange marmalade and jam, saving the peel for candied sweets, which the children devoured. Believe it or not, even schmaltz was prepared on Chanukah for Pesach because geese were fattest that time of year. Griebene with matzah and a glass of tea was a special evening meal they ate with relish. Russel borsht, left in barrels to age, was relished during Pesach, and eaten along with a plate of boiled potatoes.

Today, a wide variety of Kosher Le'Pesach products is available and yom tov is a lot easier than it was in Israel in 1930. Pesach kasher v'sameyach!

P

GEBROCHTS

fluffiest matzah balls

*These are really the fluffiest kneidlach. The batter should have a
creamy consistency; it should not be stiff.*

4 eggs	generous pinch of pepper
3 tablespoons oil	4 tablespoons seltzer
1 teaspoon salt	1 cup matzah meal, scant

Beat eggs until light and frothy. Stir in oil, salt, pepper, and seltzer. Stir
in matzah meal. The mixture should be the consistency of sour cream.
Let stand for about 15 minutes to thicken. Bring a large pot of water
to boil. Form mixture into balls and drop into boiling water. Simmer
covered for 40 minutes or longer.

Yields about 16 balls.

VARIATION

7–Up or Sprite can be used instead of plain seltzer. For richer flavor,
add 1–2 teaspoons chicken soup mix to mixture.

ⓜ

meat blintzes

These non-gebrochts blintz leaves can also be filled with chicken,
vegetables, or cheese.

BLINTZ LEAVES

4 eggs

1 tablespoon oil

1½ cups water

9 tablespoons potato starch

1 teaspoon salt

oil, for frying

FILLING

1 large onion, sliced

3 tablespoons oil

3 cups (leftover) cooked meat, cut
  into chunks

1 small potato, cooked

⅓ teaspoon salt

¼ teaspoon black pepper

pinch of cinnamon

3 tablespoons meat gravy or water

Lightly beat eggs for blintz leaves. Add oil and 1 cup water. Combine remaining water with potato starch and salt. Mix everything together until smooth. Pour a little oil into a hot skillet to cover bottom. Pour in 2 or 3 tablespoons of batter and tilt skillet to spread. Fry until brown along the sides. Turn over and fry an additional minute. Turn over onto a clean cloth. Stir batter after making each blintz leaf.

When the blintz leaves are done, sauté onion for filling in oil. In a food processor with a blade, process meat, potato, and sautéed onions. Add salt, pepper, and cinnamon. Add a few spoonfuls of gravy or water to achieve the right consistency. Place 1 tablespoonful of filling on each blintz leaf. Fold over and roll into a blintz. Fry in a hot skillet until brown on both sides. Serve warm with meat gravy.

Yields 14–16 blintzes.

TIP

Refrigerating batter for half an hour before
frying will prevent blintzes from becoming
rubbery.

GEBROCHTS

matzah nut stuffing

*Matzah, vegetables, nuts, and spices come together in this easy
recipe to create a delicious, satisfying stuffing.*

6 matzahs, broken into small pieces ⅓ teaspoon pepper
1 large onion, sliced 1 teaspoon paprika
½ green pepper, diced 2 eggs, beaten
½ cup oil 1 medium onion, chopped
⅔ cup mushrooms, sliced, optional ½ cup coarsely chopped almonds,
1 teaspoon salt, or to taste   optional

Soak matzah in hot water until soft and then squeeze out water. Sauté
sliced onion and green pepper in oil until onion is tender. Stir in mushrooms and sauté an additional 5 minutes, until onions are golden. Remove from heat and stir in the matzah, salt, pepper, paprika, eggs,
chopped onion, and almonds.

Yields enough stuffing for a 5-pound chicken.

VARATION

Omit the sautéing and the mushrooms. Chop the large onion and
combine with remaining ingredients.

Can also be baked in a greased baking dish, adding 2 more beaten
eggs to the mixture.

GEBROCHTS

pesach apple kugel

Simple, classic, and delicious.

6 eggs
1 cup sugar
juice of 1 lemon or 1 small orange
1 teaspoon grated lemon rind,
    optional
½ cup oil

4–5 large tart apples, shredded
1 cup matzah meal
¼ teaspoon salt
1 teaspoon cinnamon
⅓ cup coarsely chopped nuts
½–⅔ cup light raisins, optional

Beat together eggs and sugar. Add juice, lemon rind, oil, apples, matzah meal, salt, cinnamon, nuts, and raisins, if desired. Pour into a greased 9–inch baking pan and bake at 350° for 1 hour.

Serves 8–10.

GEBROCHTS

pesach vegetable casserole

This light vegetable casserole is a welcome change from the high-protein dishes that dominate the Pesach menu.

1 large onion, diced
1 stalk celery, diced
½ cup sliced mushrooms
5 tablespoons olive oil
3–4 carrots, grated
¾ cup matzah meal

16 ounces frozen chopped spinach,
    thawed and drained
3 eggs, beaten
1½ teaspoons salt
¼ teaspoon pepper

Sauté onions, celery, and mushrooms in oil until tender. Remove from heat. Stir in remaining ingredients. Pour mixture into a well-greased loaf pan and bake in a preheated 350° oven for 45 minutes.

Serves 10–12.

GEBROCHTS

pesach onion kugel

This unique kugel is a hit every time it's served.

6 eggs
2 cups chopped onion
⅓ cup oil

½ cup matzah meal
1¼ teaspoons salt
¼ teaspoon pepper

Beat eggs until light. Stir in onions, oil, matzah meal, salt, and pepper. Pour into a well-oiled 14x5-inch loaf pan. Bake in a preheated 375° oven for 35–40 minutes.

Serves 8–10.

GEBROCHTS

pesach vegetable loaf

An enjoyable side dish for a fleishig meal.

1 large onion, diced
3 tablespoons oil
3½ cups sliced celery
3 medium carrots, shredded
1 green pepper, diced
½ red pepper, diced
⅔ cup sliced mushrooms

3–4 tablespoons water
4 eggs, beaten
1 medium potato, grated
1 cup matzah meal
2 teaspoons salt
½ teaspoon pepper

Sauté onion in oil for 5 minutes. Add celery, carrots, green and red pepper, and mushrooms. Continue sautéeing, covered, on low heat until tender-crisp, adding water halfway through. In a bowl, combine eggs, potato, sautéed vegetables, matzah meal, salt, and pepper. Pour into a well-greased 11x4-inch loaf pan. Bake in a preheated 375° oven for 50 minutes. Serve hot.

Serves 10.

GEBROCHTS

pesach kishke

This kishke can be put into your cholent or baked in the oven to be served as a side dish.

1½ cups matzah meal

2 stalks celery, chopped

1 medium potato, shredded

3 tablespoons cold water

1 large onion, diced

½ cup oil

1 teaspoon salt

⅓ teaspoon pepper

Combine all ingredients. Wrap well in baking paper and place on top of cholent, immersed partly in the water. Cook in cholent overnight. Or place in a greased baking pan and bake covered in a preheated 350° oven for 1 hour.

Serves 8–10.

NON-GEBROCHTS

sweet potatoes with dried fruit

In our home, this is a regular dish for the yom tov day meal that follows the seder.

1 16-ounce can pineapple tidbits, with juice

1 cup cold water

½ cup honey or sugar

juice of 1 lemon

¼ teaspoon salt

2 tablespoons potato starch

2–3 medium sweet potatoes, peeled and sliced

1½ cups sliced carrots

1 cup pitted dried prunes

1 cup dried apricots

In a saucepan, combine liquid from pineapple can, water, sugar, lemon juice, and salt. Dissolve potato flour in the mixture and then cook, while stirring, until thickened, about 2 minutes. In a 9x12-inch baking pan, place sweet potatoes, carrots, pineapple tidbits, prunes, and apricots. Pour sauce on top. Cover and bake in a preheated 350° oven for 25 minutes. Remove cover and bake another 20–25 minutes.

Serves 8–10.

GEBROCHTS

classic pesach sponge cake

This cake is a success every time you bake it. Leave it plain, cut it into layers and fill it, or ice it with your favorite icing and sprinkle toasted slivered almonds or shredded coconut on top. I still recall making this sponge cake in a Wonder Pot when I first came to Israel many years ago, before I had a Pesachdig oven, and even then it was a hit!

9 large eggs, separated

1½ cups sugar

⅓ cup oil

juice and grated rind of 1 lemon

1 teaspoon vanilla extract

¼ teaspoon salt

½ cup Pesach cake meal

½ cup potato starch

Beat egg yolks until light and thick, slowly adding ¾ cup sugar. Add oil, lemon juice, grated lemon rind, vanilla, and salt. Blend in cake meal and potato starch. In another bowl, beat egg whites, gradually adding ¾ cup sugar until stiff. Fold into egg yolk mixture. Pour into a greased 10-inch tube pan. Bake in a preheated 350° oven for 1 hour. Turn upside down to cool.

Serves 10–12.

VARIATIONS

Chocolate Nut Sponge Cake: Add 5 tablespoons cocoa and ⅓ cup chopped nuts to yolk mixture. Omit lemon juice and rind.

Orange Juice Sponge Cake: Add juice and grated rind of 1 large orange instead of lemon.

GEBROCHTS

pesach angel food cake

A light, fluffy, egg–white only cake,
good for those cholesterol–intake watchers.

9 large eggs, whites only
¼ teaspoon salt
3 tablespoons lemon juice
1½ cups sugar

¼ cup Pesach cake meal or fine
matzah meal
¾ cup potato starch

Beat egg whites until frothy. Add salt and lemon juice. Gradually add
sugar and beat until stiff peaks form. Fold in cake meal, potato starch,
and remaining sugar. Pour mixture into a greased 10-inch tube pan.
Bake in preheated 350° oven for 50–60 minutes. Remove from oven
and turn pan upside down on top of soda bottle to cool.

VARIATION:

Non-Gebrochts Angel Food Cake: Omit cake meal or matzah meal
and use 1 scant cup potato starch.

TIP

For a good furniture polish, combine the juice
of 1 lemon with 1 teaspoon olive oil and 1
teaspoon water. It cleans and preserves
wood furniture.

GEBROCHTS

pesach date and nut cake

A deliciously fruity, nutty Pesach cake that your family will love.

7 eggs, separated
1 cup sugar
juice and grated rind of 1 lemon
½ cup potato starch
⅓ cup Pesach cake meal

¼ teaspoon salt
1½ cups chopped dates
½ cup chopped nuts
1 teaspoon cinnamon

Beat egg yolks for 3 minutes, gradually adding ½ cup sugar. Stir in grated lemon juice and rind. Blend in potato starch, cake meal, and salt. Stir in chopped dates, nuts, and cinnamon. Beat egg whites until frothy, gradually add remaining sugar, and beat until stiff. Fold into yolk mixture. Pour into a greased 10-inch tube apan or 9x13-inch baking pan. Bake in a preheated 350° oven for 50 minutes if using a tube pan and for 40 minutes if using a rectangular pan.

Serves 10–12.

NON-GEBROCHTS

pesach brownies

Be careful not to overbake these incredible non-gebrochts brownies.
They are amazingly luscious and moist, and very popular.

4 eggs
1¾ cups sugar
1 cup oil
½ cup cocoa

¾ cup potato starch
1 cup walnuts, coarsely chopped
1 teaspoon vanilla extract, or ½
   teaspoon vanilla sugar

Beat eggs, gradually adding sugar. Stir in remaining ingredients. Pour mixture into a greased 9x13-inch baking pan. Bake in a preheated 350° oven for 25–30 minutes. Sprinkle chopped nuts on top before baking for a special look.

Yields 24 brownies.

GEBROCHTS

pesach nut pie crust

Use this crust with a variety of fillings.

½ cup matzah meal
½ cup finely chopped almonds
3 tablespoons sugar

pinch of salt
¼ cup oil
1 egg white, slightly beaten

Combine all the ingredients thoroughly. Pat on bottom and sides of a 9-inch pie pan. Bake in a preheated 350° oven for 20–25 minutes.

GEBROCHTS

pesach lemon pie

This is a favorite Pesach dessert in my home. It keeps well in the refrigerator and can also be served when company drops by.

PIE CRUST

1 cup matzah meal
⅓ cup oil
¼ teaspoon salt
½ teaspoon cinnamon
3 tablespoons sugar

FILLING

1 cup sugar
2 cups cold water
3 tablespoons potato starch

3 egg yolks
1 tablespoon oil
pinch of salt
juice of 2 large lemons
2 teaspoons grated lemon rind
½ teaspoon vanilla extract

MERINGUE TOPPING

3 egg whites
¼ cup sugar
½ teaspoon vanilla extract

To prepare the crust, mix together matzah meal, oil, salt, cinnamon, and sugar until smooth. Let rest for 10 minutes. Pat evenly on the bottom and sides of a greased 9-inch pie pan, bringing the dough up to the rim evenly. Bake about 12 minutes in a preheated 350° oven until light brown. To prepare the filling, combine sugar and water in a saucepan and bring to a boil. Lower heat. In a small bowl, dissolve potato starch in a little cold water and pour slowly into simmering sugar mixture, stirring until it thickens. In a small bowl, beat egg yolks with a fork. Add 3 tablespoons of the hot mixture to the egg yolks and then stir the yolks into the cooking mixture. Cook for 5 minutes until smooth and creamy. Remove from heat and stir in oil, salt, lemon juice, and lemon rind. Let cool. Pour mixture into the baked crust. Prepare meringue: Beat egg whites until stiff, gradually adding ¼ cup sugar and vanilla. Spread evenly on top of filling. Brown in a preheated 350° oven for 10–15 minutes.

Serves 8–9.

VARIATION

Instead of meringue, spread top evenly with whipped cream and decorate with strawberry halves.

GEBROCHTS

pesach apple pie

An old-fashioned dessert, adapted here for Pesach.

CRUST
2 eggs
1 cup sugar
¾ cup oil
¼ teaspoon salt
½ cup potato starch
½ cup matzah meal

FILLING
6–7 large apples, thinly sliced

½ cup raisins
1 teaspoon cinnamon
⅓ cup sugar
⅓ cup coarsely chopped nuts,
    optional
4 tablespoons strawberry jam
3 tablespoons matzah meal

GLAZE
1 egg yolk, beaten with 1 teaspoon
    water

Beat eggs and sugar for crust. Stir in remaining ingredients and continue mixing until the mixture forms a dough. Pat ⅔ of the mixture into a greased 9-inch pie pan. In a separate bowl, combine apples, raisins, cinnamon, sugar, nuts, and 3 tablespoons strawberry jam. Stir in matzah meal. Spread 1 tablespoon strawberry jam on crust. Pour apple mixture over the jam. Spread remaining ⅓ of crust on top. Brush glaze on top. Bake in a preheated 350° oven for about 50 minutes until golden brown.

Serves 8.

NON-GEBROCHTS

pesach sherbet

This recipe can be used for Pesach or all year round. It is colorful,
delicious, and nutritious.

3 cups water

1½ cups sugar

1 cup orange or pink grapefruit
  juice

1 cup chopped kiwi, pureed in a
  food processor

1 cup chopped strawberries, pureed
  in a food processor

Combine water and sugar in a saucepan and bring to a boil. Simmer for
a minute or two. Combine 1 cup of hot sugar-water with orange or pink
grapefruit juice; combine 1 cup of hot sugar-water with kiwi; and 1 cup
with strawberries. Pour each mixture into a separate, small plastic container. Freeze until firm. Remove from freezer and slightly process each
color separately in a food processor. Spoon or scoop layers of alternating
colors into individual serving dishes or stemware.

Serves 12.

VARIATION

Use other fruit in place of kiwi or strawberries, such as apples, pears,
or blueberries.

TIP

To make a delicious and nutritious drink for
children, put 2 scoops of ice cream in a glass of
fruit juice and mix until smooth.

ⓟ

NON-GEBROCHTS

fresh peach whip

A delightful, light dessert! When preparing it for dieters, omit the whipped topping.

2 cups fresh peaches, cut up
¾ cup sugar
1 tablespoon lemon juice
2 egg whites

1 8-ounce container dessert topping, optional
fresh sliced peaches, or cherries, for
garnish, optional

In a large mixer bowl, combine peaches, sugar, lemon juice, and egg whites. Beat for 3 minutes on low speed, then continue on high speed for an additional 10–15 minutes. Volume will increase considerably, to nearly triple the size. If using commercial whipped topping, whip in a separate bowl and remove a scant cup of this whipped topping to dab on top of finished dessert. Fold remainder into the whipped peach mixture. Pour into a container and freeze.

When ready to serve, scoop peach whip into glass dessert dishes. Garnish with a dab of whipped topping, a slice of fresh peach, or a whole cherry. Instead of pouring into a container, you can spoon the mixture into the dessert dishes, garnish as above, and then freeze.

Serves 12.

=== T I P ===

To remove tarnish from copper, stainless steel, and brass, make a paste out of lemon juice and baking soda or salt, and apply to tarnished surface. Leave on for 5 minutes and rub off.

GEBROCHTS

pesach mandelbrodt

*The year-round classic in its Pesachdig version. I still remember
my Bubby enjoying this scrumptious treat with a glass of tea on
Shabbos afternoon.*

3 eggs	½ cup Pesach cake meal
¾ cup sugar	½ cup potato starch
¾ cup oil	⅔ cup slivered almonds
¼ teaspoon salt	½ cup sugar, for sprinkling
juice and rind of ½ a lemon	1 teaspoon cinnamon, for sprinkling

Beat eggs until light, adding sugar, oil, salt, lemon juice, and lemon
rind. Stir in cake meal, potato starch, and almonds. Spread batter in
a greased 9x12-inch baking pan. Bake in a 350° oven for 35 minutes.
While still warm, cut into mandelbrodt strips. Return slices to baking
pan. Combine sugar and cinnamon and sprinkle on top. Bake for an
additional 20 minutes.

Yields about 30 slices.

NON-GEBROCHTS

chocolate-dipped coconut bonbons

A delicious non-gebrochts recipe for those who do not use potato flour on Pesach. Indulge your family with these delicious homemade treats!

4 cups shredded coconut
2 cups sifted powdered
    sugar
¾ cup mashed potatoes

2 cups chocolate chips or broken
    chocolate
6 tablespoons margarine
1 teaspoon vanilla extract

Combine coconut, powdered sugar, and mashed potatoes. Refrigerate about 2 hours or overnight until firm. Form into balls about 1 inch in diameter. Place on a platter or pan and refrigerate 1½ hours. Melt chocolate chips and combine with margarine and vanilla. Add 1 tablespoon of water if mixture is too thick. Dip each coconut ball in warm chocolate mixture. Chill and serve.

Yields about 24 balls.

=TIP=

To make a delicious and nutritious drink for children, put 2 scoops of ice cream in a glass of fruit juice and mix until smooth.

INDEX